Praise for *The Blackberry Tea Club*

"Barbara Herrick wears the middle years of her life with class, grace, and phenomenal insight. She takes readers on a glorious romp down a raging Idaho river, ponders the complexities of her fifty-something mirrored self, and takes time to reflect on those personal decisions that most affected her life and loves, pain and celebrations."

—JUDY WARE, PH.D.,
conflict resolution facilitator and writer

"Barbara Herrick's book illuminates the joyful possibilities of being a woman growing older in America today. It overflows with the sheer bliss of being alive."

—ROSEMARY CUNNINGHAM,
author of *Fifty Ways to Feed Your Soul*

"Barbara does a wonderful job of reframing who we women of the 21st century are becoming and how we got there. And she does it in a manner that combines self-help, inspiration, and memoir all in one. *The Blackberry Tea Club* defies genre by being intimate and personal while imparting a perspective that challenges widely-held beliefs about what comes with aging. And these are the very beliefs that often become self-fulfilling prophecies that send otherwise healthy, vibrant women to therapists' offices for fear of being abnormal, or worse, trapped in futures they find unbearable."

—MARSHA L. ROBERTS, PH.D.,
psychologist

"Barbara Herrick's voice is as original and real as the mountains, rivers, and farm country of her beloved Idaho. Her recollections include a grand ride with the tea club members down the Payette River, a clever yet universal foray into ham salad that is regularly punctuated by comments from the 'Matriarchs,' and an extraordinarily true-to-the-bone exploration of her family health – physical and mental – adding up to a map of the woman complete with a self-study report on her flesh that is at once both funny and honest. Hers is an autobiography of body and soul, 'miswhacks' and wonders that make the glory years a time of fulfillment and fancy."

—ALAN MINSKOFF,
author of *Blue Ink Runs Out on a Partly Cloudy Day*

"Barbara Herrick's *The Blackberry Tea Club* is a heartfelt exploration of an American life that is funny, tender, and graceful. Fraught with gentle lessons, it conveys stone-cold facts of the human condition and teaches us that the Blackberry Tea Club is a society we can all enjoy if we are lucky enough to share Herrick's intriguing and positive perspective on the aging process."

—COLLEEN BIRCH MAILE,
editor, *SkyWest Magazine*

"Barbara Herrick writes from her heart, spins words of pure silk, and invites every woman to go for the gold. Hers is a story that bounces through the perilous rapids of early life to discover sublime waters in the middle years. Instead of feeling maligned and misunderstood when arriving *at that certain age*, readers will celebrate with Barbara who offers a refreshing map for self-respect. *The Blackberry Tea Club* points the way to renewed energy and buoyancy, and it does so with a giggle and a smile."

—SUSAN REULING FURNESS, M.ED.,
marriage and family therapist, seasoned middle-ager
and contributing author of *The Writing Group Book*

The Blackberry Tea Club

The
Blackberry Tea Club
Women in Their Glory Years

Barbara Herrick

CONARI PRESS

First published in 2004 by Conari Press,
an imprint of Red Wheel/Weiser, LLC
York Beach, ME

With offices at:
500 Third Street, Suite 230
San Francisco, CA 94107
www.redwheelweiser.com

Library of Congress Cataloging-in-Publication Data

Herrick, Barbara.
  The Blackberry Tea Club : women in their glory years / Barbara Herrick.
    p. cm.
  ISBN 1-57324-965-3
  1. Middle aged women. 2. Middle aged women – Idaho – Biography. I. Title.
  HQ1059.4.H47 2004
  305.244 – dc22   2004005874

Book design by Maxine Ressler
Typeset in Fournier and Avenir

Printed in Canada
TCP

8   7   6   5   4

To the Matriarchs in the Sky:
Lorene Evans Herrick,
Belle Evans, Hazel Herrick,
Frances Evans, Tiny Evans, Lily Westfall,
Bernice Herrick, Nira Bond.

And to the Matriarchs still solidly with us:
Rita Brilz, Pearl Cox, Nina Parks, Ruth Wright.

Thank You

To Jan Johnson, Kate Hartke, Jill Rogers, and Brenda Knight of Conari Press who opened the doors of possibility and to Dorian Gossy, Kathleen Fivel, and Maxine Ressler for the art of bookmaking.

To my beloved friends and family: Steve Herrick and Maggie Brilz, Julie Herrick, Tanya Johnson, Mark Brilz and Karl Bigler, Bob and JoAnn Andrew, Alan and Royanne Minskoff, Steven and Pam Mayfield, Richard and Judith Steele, Tom and Colleen Maile, Jeanette Germain and Marshall Brown, Mike Christian and Jennifer Marcus, Carol Gerber Allred and Brian Flay, Mike and Marty Downey, Gail Farley and Tod Palmer, Sherry Grabowski, Gina Phillips, Diane Ronayne and Gary Richardson, Marsha Roberts, Mary Owen and Norman Weinstein, Alison Isenberg, Mollie O'Shea, Peggy Farnworth, Tim and Sue Furness, Jim and Judy Ware, Carolyn Barbier and Chip Calamaio, Ellie McKinnon and Roger Kynaston, Sharon Hanson, Jan Alden and Jim Church, Joan Logghe, Kathy Barrett, Juanita Hepler, Gwynne McElhinney and

Robert McAndrew, Robin Young, Surel Mitchell, Leslie and Dan Gunnerson, Jamie Dater, Jeanette Ullery, Susan and Don Curtis, Diana Sparks, Ellie Hilvers-Bristol, Teresa Sgalio, Vanessa Klaus, Jody Gibson, Barbara Ross, Pam Spickelmeier, Mike and Lisa Wahowski, Chris Dempsey, John Rember, Tish Thornton, Bill and Judy Studebaker, Gino Sky, Jamie Armstrong, Robert Whitlatch, Rick Ardinger, David Sample, Paul Collins, and Linda Stout.

To my extended families: The Evans, the Marvins, the Westfalls, the Herricks, the Bonds, the Parks, the Johnsons, the Brilz, the Jackman-Hendricks.

To the Log Cabin Literary Center and Fishtrap: two delicious writers' communities in the West.

To the beloved man
Keith C. Herrick

To the grandest man
Kenneth O. Herrick

Mackenzie Herrick and Scott Herrick
The reason for everything

Contents

She who reconciles the ill-matched threads
of her life, and weaves them gratefully into a single cloth —
it's she who drives the loudmouths from the hall
and clears it for a different celebration

where the one guest is you.
In the softness of evening
it's you she receives.

You are the partner of her loneliness,
the unspeaking center of her monologues.
With each disclosure you encompass more
and she stretches beyond what limits her,
to hold you.

—RAINER MARIA RILKE

Glory Years

We enter our Glory Years full tilt, our heads and hearts high.
Our midyears are when
we finally find our place and our peace,
when we are powerful, when we are well and well-rewarded,
when we're the best at what we do,
when we discover that life is good,
and we are good in it.

Our minds are deep and clear,
our hearts are fierce and full,
our souls unafraid.
Whether we are alone, in tandem or in family,
whether we are scientists, artists, nurturers, or activists,
or all of those things at once,
whether we have achieved all of our dreams
or are just beginning to find them,
whether life has been fair or whether it has not,
we know our strength, our spirit, our will, and our direction.

WE TRUST OUR BODIES.
Striding in long lengths across our chosen paths, we walk.
We swim in deep waters.
We delight in a stunning red dress and sexy three-inch heels,
but we won't wear them long —
we have places to go that require a wilderness of
spirit and shoes to match.
Knowing pain and loss,
ache and misspent hope,
we have survived our own lives
and found a pathway that sustains us.
Pleasure is ours for the taking:
the feel of warm sand on bare feet,
what a gin and tonic can do for a hot August afternoon,
the feel of silk on bare skin,
what a good man's hand can do for a Sunday morning.

WE TRUST OUR MINDS.

Gathering in quilting groups and reading groups,
we talk over creamy coffee or blackberry tea
or a purple wine, dark and mysterious as the ways of the world.
And talk. And talk.
And talk.
Taking in ideas, throwing them out,
working them over until we understand in our bones.
Gossip loses its salacious edge.
It's not that we don't talk about people, we do.
But our gossip arises from our care for people
and what happens to them.
When we bump into an old friend on a walk,
and she tells us of her recent divorce and surgery,
a question we are most likely to ask is this:
What are you reading that helps you through this?
We are transported by painting and sculpture,
by dance and poetry, by music.
We are drawn to the arts as dreamers and creators,
because we are sure of what we have to say.
We are drawn to the sciences because we are
hungry for the why of the why of things.
We are drawn to politics and business because
we can no longer be turned away from those endeavors and
because those institutions desperately need us.
Always we teach. Always we nurture. Always we mentor.

WE TRUST OUR HEARTS.
No longer disdainful of our own tears,
we cry easily and often, in pleasure and in pain.
We laugh over our own lunacies and indulge other people
as they sort out their own.
We are intense in our loyalties and our passions;
our friendships are sustained over decades;
as is our work, our art.
A child can rend our heart, as can an honest man.
We have an ever-growing capacity for joy.
Life, more often than not, seems
mysterious, fragile, intensely beautiful,
terrible in its consequences, blessed in its graces.

WE ARE SPIRITUAL.
Either sustaining our traditions with a quiet absoluteness,
or finding another that serves us better.
Some of us may have thrown off the traces and
walked barefoot around the world.
We believe in angels, either the sublime beings,
or in the more unsentimental angels: each other.
We pray.
We trust great intuitive leaps, the power of love,
a sensibility of gratitude, and a profound acceptance
of life as it is.
Our kindness is as a state of grace.

WE ARE NOT AMUSED

by drugs or the abuse of alcohol.
We are not amused by the lack of funding for education
or the lack of protection for unwed mothers.
We are not amused by hungry children in our own city.
We are not amused by people who neglect or
abuse their own bodies or any other.
Nor are we amused by an overt and degrading sexuality
foisted on the most vulnerable of our daughters.
We are wearied by war, knowing that it implodes,
as well as explodes,
destroying its makers as well as its victims.
We know what needs to be done.
We will do it.

WE TRUST OUR UNHAPPINESS.

Whether in relationships that confine us or
jobs that demean us,
we find that depression or anxiety are based on
real factors in our lives.
We reject the notion that something is wrong with us,
and embrace the knowing that something is wrong.
We will attend to it, rather than continue to bleed
emotionally, physically, spiritually, financially.

WE LOVE OUR MEN.

They have literally given us life,
and we honor our husbands and our fathers for that.
Our brothers have sharpened our sense of humor, made us
giggle at unlikely times, shared a sense of adventure,
been our best friends, our most enduring conspirators.
We may have married young or waited a while.
We might have tossed out the men who were
marginal, confining, mean, or untrustworthy.
We might have found a true gem
who needed no polishing,
or we might have found a sturdy fixer-upper
and done our best with him.
We might have had one true love, or
learned to love in sequence
or in total.
At some critical point we learned to love
our old guys in a whole new way.
We can sustain friendships with men
that are not sexual,
and we can leer with the best of them.
We love our sexuality, as it comes these days
from a deep biology,
from our most interior selves.
Sex is no longer skin-deep
and in our Glory Years,
we are interesting lovers.

WE ARE BEAUTIFUL.

Beauty is no longer one-dimensional nor unachievable.
We are beautiful no matter what shape our bodies.
The lines in our faces soften our countenances.
Our silvering hair forms halos around our faces.
We exude light and energy, intellect and will,
passion and folly, pleasure and pain, strength and
a little bit of magic.
We have reinstalled the stars in our eyes.

WE ARE MOTHERS,

nourishing and nurturing the children who were born to us
and the ones who were not, the ones within our families,
and the ones within the larger family that inhabits our Earth.
We trace our heartbeat back to our mother's heartbeat,
to her mother's heartbeat, and to the mother before that
until we reach clear back and sense
our first mother's heartbeat
and the breath of Mama God.
That original energy is ours,
the gift and heritage of spirit and biology.
Our power is broad and deep, and the world is changing
because of our touch, our words, our breath, our pulse.
We know that the control over our own lives extends
no further than our fingertips,
but that our influence is infinite.

WE CHOOSE OUR FOREVERS CAREFULLY.

Coming to Our Senses

THE RIVER is a torrent, constrained by the great brown hills that surround us and the black megaliths that jut against a sky so blue my heart hurts. The Blackberry Tea Club, four women in our Glory Years, is on an outing, a two-day float trip through world-class rapids on the south fork of the Payette River in central Idaho. The water, still snowfed in August, is so cold it takes the breath, while the air temperature sits at ninety-four degrees on the flats above the canyons. It's hotter here on the surface of the water, where the rock walls cradle the heat.

What's a body to do with extremes like that?

Burly water, mountain cold, crashes over my head and shoulders, streams down my back, sends our raft careening. "Dig!" Sam yells. "Starboard! Pull! Hard!" We lean far over the side of the raft, our legs straddling the tubes, bodies balanced in midair. Our paddling straightens the raft just in time to shoot over a wave the size of the monsters in my last dream and then slips us into a hole that would spin the raft for a God-induced eternity, given its keeper nature. The water clobbers us, thrashes the breath from our lungs. Cold water in the crotch is a whoop in the making. I stare into a trough of glassy, green water. Paddling white water is paddling froth; green water is hard and real as cement. To propel the raft you have to paddle deep enough to touch the green – otherwise you have no purchase on power.

And you need to do it with the deep, spiritual connection between people that allows for concerted action in the absence of words. A metaphor, I'm thinking. I laugh and shout from the base of my lizard brain: Pay attention! Stay with the moment! Stay here! Mind-traveling in the middle of Wang-doodle Rapids is deadly.

We dig deep – Sam shouting what to do and when to do it – spiral the green around our paddles, pull free from the keeper hole, and slip through the turbulence into a relatively peaceful stretch of water.

My hair is plastered to the sides of my head. My fifty-year-old body has taken a drenching. There is no way to hide these wide flamboyant breasts under my wet T-shirt. I am free of makeup and the ignoble trappings of my tiny life. This river washes me clean of prissiness and pretension.

Three other boats are with us, but clearly we have the liveliest crew. We all lead responsible, respectable lives:

Sherry is all heart, too open sometimes for the challenges she faces as director of an intensive care unit in a large medical center. She has an amazing mind – with photographic recall, she remembers everything she's read. Gail is the leader, a strategist, the woman with long strides and an unerring sense of direction. She finds refuge in her garden – the fact that she views the whole Earth as her garden gives her a remarkable equanimity. Marty is a healer, by trade a coronary care nurse and a professor of holistic nursing, but she's onto something deeper and more vital. There's no holding her back. She's searching out the mysteries of a body deeply attached to a soul and reporting back. I am Miss Priss, the poet, and there is no accounting for my mysteries. But out here, we lose our "herlady-ma'amship-diva-ship-highpriestess-poetess" selves. We giggle and scream and ride the wild waters.

We've been friends for ten years, last count, starting with conversations late at night at a bar where we sipped Blackberry Tea – a lovely ferment of amaretto, Grand Marnier, and blackberry tea. We talk children, men, jobs, weight, clothes, food, travel, gossip, politics, medicine, healing, spirituality, adventure, books – the works.

We've taken to these conversations and now these extremes with the exuberance of twelve year olds. After each set of rapids we smack the water hard with our paddles, then crack them overhead and hoot with adrenaline joy. A stranger hearing us would be hard-pressed to guess that two of us are in our forties, and the other two have reached our fifties: grand old broads riding high.

Sam is our river guide, a stunning man in his late twenties: a longish mane of golden hair, the lean body of an Olympian, a kind heart and a lively mind. He is utterly at home with four women in their Glory Years. His mama has done a sterling job with him and we advise him to tell her so. When we ask him if he'll tell her about us, he laughs and says, "Ohhh, yeahhh!" Melvin is our sixteen-year-old safety kayaker whose stories around the campfire all begin with *"There I was . . . ."* For six weeks the previous winter, he kayaked in Chile. Melvin took a hundred dollars with him, lavished ninety-two of it on ice cream and eight on a necklace made by an Indian woman. The rate of exchange being what it is, Melvin ate a lot of ice cream.

Old father Freud thought that the benchmark of maturity was the ability to delay gratification and pleasure: to refrain from eating ninety-two dollars worth of ice cream; to sway only slightly with the music when it wafts through us; to resist riding the wild waters or taking trails that lead us out of plain sight; to wait to paint rainbows on our faces or in our minds.

But Glory Years women may well have a different opinion; all that delaying has had its due. What drives us now is the sensibility that we are aging, and if we're to enjoy our remaining time, something drastic has to change – beginning with our minds. Maybe old talents we've ignored finally have their way with us; a cause beckons to us, or travel takes us down foreign roads. Perhaps something jars us loose from the ruts we've dug into our minds; we might be newly sober – or newly sane. Maybe we've suffered a profound loss or a real defeat. Or the things (often with a high gunk factor) we've stuffed into back corridors of our hearts and our heads refuse to stay put any longer and come forward with embarrassing force. Certainly we are starved for joy. Absolutely we are surprised by love.

Sometime during our Glory Years, our soul leaps from the moorings of what has been. Often people, the teensiest bit arrogant, especially if they haven't gone through it, call this a midlife crisis. It is not a crisis. It is a passage into the authentic: intense, concrete, and predictable as green, glassy water on its way through a narrow, black canyon. It is a spiritual passage. It is an emotional imperative.

We follow the haunting songs of this new siren. She beckons us and we swim in deep waters. Instead of death on the rocks, we find a life in the music. Our adamant need for pleasure is a coming to our senses, a coming to life of our eyes, ears, tongue, fingers, and skin. We are called by something as serious as joy.

We want Emily Dickinson's encounter with the long grasses and buttercups around her home: "To live is so startling it leaves little time for anything else."

Old jokes, funny instances, rampant silliness, and adren-aline-adventures break us free from the cycle of grayness. But we won't stop there. We're hard on the lookout for something more. We want an unconstrained enchantment. The good news is this: joy arises from the most central, per-sonal tasks of our lives. We need not destroy our families or hike barefoot around the world, carrying no more than an odd obsession or two. We need not go any further than the outside edge of our own skin or the most tentative edges of our hearts.

We yearn for a bliss that is an intimacy with meaning. We want the sensibility that our lives are ripe with signifi-cance, that our *every days* are deeper metaphors, that we are fraught with portent. It is joyous to mean something to the world around us, to engage the most profound part of ourselves in the act of living.

We're *Stalking Joy,* as the poet Margaret Benbow wrote. It's now or never.

Just around noon, we eddy up in a stretch of river, calm as a quilt, and unload our gear. We need to portage around a massive double falls. The sound of dangerous water is nearby. We stretch out on wobbly legs, unsteady from grip-ping the side of the tubes for three or so hours. Oh boy, do I have to pee, and I take full advantage of the wading. Others boaters head up what is euphemistically called a trail. Most of the trek is uphill, but fortunately the ascent is low and slow. The trouble is this: there is no dirt, only a field of rocks that tilt and adjust themselves under our weight – slag from gold mining spills over the whole side of a seven-story mountain. Gold brought people to these wary, weary hills, and their tailings are a geological history.

When Buffy Sainte-Marie wrote, "You have to sniff out joy, keep your nose to the joy-trail," this might be what she had in mind. I go carefully, thoughtfully, picking out each step, worrying that I am too slow. But slow is better than a twisted or broken ankle. Further, my slowness is an excuse for the people trailing behind to pick every step thoughtfully, too.

"Take your time," Sam shouts.

The last part of the portage is straight up, up and into a castle of white rocks the size of a city block three stories high. Scrambling toehold to toehold, I hoist my opulent girth up and over, until I stand finally on the top of the cliff and look down into the grand and the raucous, an immense cascade of water. *Big Falls*. There are two falls, one on top of the other, each as big as a bus. We have to shout to be heard, even from our vantage point. The waters are heavy, slick, crashing into white froth, then slipping over the second larger falls, whipped into a frenzied cream at the bottom. Such power takes my breath.

Sherry shouts a story that the guides have yet to hear: a few years ago friends of hers missed the eddy-up spot, and there was no returning. They went over Big Falls in a raft. They were dumped out into a hurricane of water; flooded with incomprehension and terror – and lived.

Dangerous places in the natural world have a sense of the sacred about them. There are forces on this planet I have no say about, no way with, no power over. The only appropriate response is silence, a shutting down of the mind and the mouth, the granting of an immense respect. Feelings of grandeur flood my synapses. Feeling more than a little giddy, I anchor this memory, this feeling in my breast. No one hurries us. They know how this place arrests the few adventurers lucky enough to stand here.

This part of the river feels male to me. Other flows in Idaho have the feel of the feminine about them, like the St. Joe in northern Idaho, slow and undulating, deep and ripe; the Clearwater, clear and pristine as a maiden. But this river, at this place – a massive rumble brooking no silliness, patriarchal in the respect it commands – is male: all intention, all power, all authority.

Ten or twelve river guides escort our rafts over the falls with long ropes that could reach across half a football field. The young men and women manage it all from the top of the cliffs. The empty boats are released from their moorings upstream, then drift into the current as the ropes pull them into the center of the river. The boats slip over the falls, fill with white water, tip over, careen through the turbulence, then do it again. The rafts are guided around the castle rocks carefully – the enterprise engineered as finely as a space shuttle tune-up. Finally the boats are pulled into the lagoon at the bottom of the falls. It is an exquisite performance.

We are trusting our lives to young men and women in their twenties. It feels just fine. They are beyond fit, wearing competence like they wear their bright orange life vests, stark against the natural browns of the hills and the immediate blue of the sky. Sometimes we lose track of the contrasts that make life vibrant; here they are unmistakable.

We step down gingerly from our white castle and head for the boats. After turning around for one last look, I gasp as Melvin launches his boat from the top of the white cliffs, paddling thin air, flying like the eagle he is, then arcing toward the river, sprawling the water with a thump. Only after he lands do I realize I've been laughing and crying, praying without a prayer, singing without a song, catching my breath and sputtering with delight.

A few years ago, I chose my own portage point, the time and the place where I eddied up, took everything I owned on my own back, walked on wobbly legs over fields of rocks that tipped and slanted, and headed straight up, looking for castles in the air. It all began as a change of mind, a shift of spirit.

I'd been managing a learning and conference center in a hospital, the one Marty, Gail, and Sherry are attached to. As hospitals go, it is certainly a good one, perhaps even a great hospital, but the physicians, nurses, and therapists who worked there were in a spiritual disrepair. Pain was etched into faces lined with exhaustion and depletion from too many hours, very ill people, constraints of time, resources, and paperwork – the villain of modern medicine. We were all living in the *more, better, faster* paradigm, not particularly indigenous to hospitals, and it was taking a huge toll on health and mood. Everyone seemed caught up in a cultural angst; the two to fourteen minutes they were allowed with each patient was eating at their sensibility of right and wrong, their imperative to take care of seriously ill people with some measure of thoughtfulness, kindness, patience, and mastery.

"That's life," we'd say, but we were a little wrong. It was only life in one place, in one instant. Life is bigger, more dangerous, alluring, and startling than we knew. We only had a glimpse of life, a sliver of life, such as it was.

One Sunday morning I'd gone to church, a New Thought church I'd escaped to while my own church sorted out what it wanted to be. This service was held in a Jewish synagogue, one of the loveliest of places, a simple 1885 Spanish revival structure. The stained glass windows drenched the inside of the synagogue with a miraculous golden light, reminiscent of the most delicate Chardonnay. The wooden benches, the altar, the cream-colored walls held a sensibility of spirit, the dignity of ancient worship. That morning local singers were playing revved-up, full-throttle, what-

I-don't-always-think-of-as gospel music songs: "It's a Wonderful World," "On the Sunny Side of the Street," "Oh
Happy Day," and "Amazing Grace."

There I was: a wandering Catholic, an itinerant Protestant, in a Jewish synagogue at a New Age church service,
singing and dancing to gospel.

Perfect.

My mind was changed in a heartbeat. *It was a wonderful
world.* This was a another point of view: that life need not
be grim. Life was possibility and endless hope – a mind-
boggling challenge to be sure; fraught with danger and portent – just like the scientists, magicians, and sages promised.

I was hungry for ice cream afterward. Black walnut ice
cream. Not ninety-two dollars worth, but enough. Gratitude
makes enough out of anything. As I sat in the winter sun
relishing every creamy bite, I was flooded with apprecia-
tion and then comprehension: A new life was about to begin.

Within six months, I left the hospital and began to write.

The morning sun light bends over the lip of the canyon
and crawls down the walls in angles and lines. I'm clutch-
ing a cup of Earl Grey, watching the steam spiral and curl
in the chill morning air. I'm bundled in a blanket, leaning
against a yellow pine which smells like butterscotch where
the sun has warmed its bark. My journal is in my lap as I
try to catch yesterday's memories before they slip away.

No one else is up, so I have the river, the edgy light, the soft moan of the ponderosas, the good humor of the chipmunks to myself.

Last night Mike, one of the river guides, was ill. His nausea was severe; he was throwing up every five or six minutes. Maybe it was food poisoning. His back and neck muscles produced spasms so tight he couldn't stand up. He was stretched out on hard ground and Marty, whose training in holistic nursing includes a heavy dose of massage therapy, pulled and kneaded the muscles in his upper back and neck until the spasms and the nausea subsided. He was pale afterwards, but moving.

I wondered about the pressure gifted young men place upon themselves. What does school do to him? Work? Are there other women as kind and as capable as Marty who can pull him out of it when it gets too bad? He might need love that does not demand much from him, love that comes as a gift.

Around the campfire last night, Miss Priss wanted to read a verse of her own. "It's a poem about bugs and sex," I said to the gathered campers. When I went to retrieve the poem, the guys shot out of camp like startled magpies. "Gotta wash up," they shouted. "Gotta get supper started." Their eighth-grade poetry lessons must have been dreadful. Either that or a fiftyish, plumpish woman reading a poem about sex might have unhinged them entirely.

It's possible.

Here's the poem, funnier then because we were drenched in mosquitoes and ants, no-see-ums and crickets, night wishes and succulent men.

Nectar Kisses
In my belly, grasshoppers zing off in
odd directions at the least distraction.

Spider's long soft legs
step lightly up the spine
leave tiny shivers on the skin.

Centipedes with their hundred feet
march to drummers of their own device,
no sensibility of another's rhythm,
an ardent chaos,
a fumbled riot,
a happy anarchy.

Don't even get me started on the ants
in my pants, crawling upwards, ever upwards.
Their tiny bites, their bitty chomps
a delicious agony.

Don't ever get me started.
Don't ever get me stopped.

Bumbled bees drone deep and soft,
carry honeyed thoughts
one slow ride at a time
to my blushed brain.

We'd settled for the night,
but the crickets take over,
a symphony of merry chirps,
crescendo until we can hardly
withstand their wild songs.

Butterflies seize my skin with nectar kisses.
They carry me away, so far away, and then
leave me limp and tumbled, hanging in midair,
weighing no more than a heartbeat.

Love drives me buggy
one shiver,
one wiggle,
one squiggle,
one merry chirp,
one buzzy flight,
one bitty chomp,
one nectar kiss
at a time.

It's later now, about six-thirty in the morning. I'm just back from a trek up the hill to the porta-potty. Sans tent, Sam, Melvin, and Mike are still asleep on a grassy slope. They've plopped down sleeping bags on hard ground – at home anywhere on earth. Young men lose their edginess, their manliness, their boisterousness in their sleep, and the innocence of little boys returns. If there is a thing that compels women, it is the sight of men sleeping . . . . They are beautiful beyond words.

Sam's long curls shine in the sunlight. Melvin's boyish face will deepen into manhood in the next year. Mike is still pale from being sick; his white skin a contrast with his dark hair and morning beard. I look at them with the conflicting emotions of the twenty-year-old lover I once was and the motherliness that comes forth now. The mother wins out. If I could kiss them on the forehead, bless them with a safe and healthy life, full of love, adventure and promise – without looking stunningly odd – I would have.

After a long, lazy breakfast we pack up and head down the river. It is a spangled day; the sun on the river is one long flash of light. The river flattens and widens into long, slow pools. We drift past meadows with lupine and buttercups, mountain grasses that smell sharp and clean and sweet. The pine and fir are spaced further apart, and the day is sweet enough for dreaming. Sometimes we catch the scent of sage on the wind. This lovely place loves us back.

We drift on wide water and watch for hawks. Sam says there's a hawk here that always waits for him, then trails along with the raft for several miles. Sure enough, we spot him and he follows us, flying from ponderosa to Douglas fir, perching long enough for us to drift by.

Soon we're in the canyon where the walls close in, where the river and the cliffs achieve an intimacy. Sam is weaving the raft down through the rocks, the way a hiker carefully picks his way over rough trail. This part of the canyon is mysterious, and we grow quiet, the way I imagine every paddler grows quiet here. The river here feels female: sage woman, lupine woman, lichen woman.

This she-river is a sculptress, carving grottoes and tunnels into basalt. The rock cliffs are close enough we can touch the sculptures, made from nonhuman forces, made from the alchemy of nature. The water must be very deep, because there are few rapids here. It's dark green, glassy and swift. The sunlight filters through the sculptured openings and leaves momentary geometric tracings on the water. The designs look like they are dancing.

All of the hollowed out places are round, smooth as sea glass, eerily symmetrical, black as crow's feathers. Small plants grow up through the rocks, careening toward sun. Flower shatters stone, as an enigmatic force as there is. This is a love unfamiliar to me.

I wonder at this odd order, this eerie beauty, this dark stone – the mystery you have to go to some effort to see, take some considerable risk. Nature here is daunting and secretive, ancient and immobile.

We have to come to Her.

"There's this bridge ahead," Sam says. "Is anybody else up for the trip?" His eyebrows raise with the question. He wants to park the raft and jump off the bridge, a feat of young men's courage. And he wants us to go with him.

Melvin, fourteen-year-old Jessica from a companion boat, and Sam are going. So are Marty, Gail, and Sherry. I watch as they climb up the bank, scamper down the bridge, and climb out over the railing. Sam leaps first, jumps a long way out; his hair is trailing sun. Then Melvin and Jessie jump, so young and ardent and brave, a little bit enamored of each other. They'll have a bond of memory, carry pieces of each other's soul as long as they live. They fly a long ways out, enter the water with a whoosh.

Then Marty, Gail, and Sherry, the grand old broads with the courage of Visigoths – nurses, mothers, wives, healers, artists, travelers – grab hands, yell "Towanda!" and leap into the air, flying like the angels they are, trusting that the river will catch them. They plunge deep into the cold current and come up screaming with exultation, boldness, and no small amount of joy. They are irrevocably in love with life, "joyously, drunkenly, serenely, divinely aware," as Henry Miller described it.

There I was, as jealous of the trip as I have been of anything in life.

When I was in my twenties, I had my wisdom teeth pulled, a happy occasion. My dentist gave me Valium and a freight load of painkillers. A goofy bliss settled in. The dentist's chair looked out over a pasture with long grasses, shaded by elms. "A beeeuuuteeeful cow, ain't it?" I remember saying.

I'm not the only woman with this experience. Candace Pert describes having a lovely summer with a bad back. "A horseback riding accident put me flat on my back in a hospital bed, doped to the gills on Talwin, a morphine derivative," she writes in her book, *Molecules of Emotion.* "There was no doubt that the drug's action in my body produced a distinctly euphoric effect, one that filled me with a bliss bordering on ecstasy."

That experience led her to question the nature of opiates and their relationship to the cells in our bodies. As a researcher in the field of psychoneuroimmunology, she, along with other scientists, discovered that our cells have little opiate receptor sites clinging to their sides, which is why opiates work one-hundred percent of the time on one-hundred percent of the people. Since living on opiates didn't seem to be a good idea, Dr. Candace wondered why those sites were there and what purpose they served in a drug-free body.

This seems like old news now, but she discovered that the body produces its own molecules of bliss: endorphins such as adrenaline and serotonin. Adrenaline is the "wahoo!" hormone; serotonin is the "ahhhhh" hormone. Those hormones hook up very nicely – thank you – to the receptor sites on the cells. When that happens, good things occur in our bodies: we gain increased feelings of well-being, a remarkable boost of energy, a sensibility of happiness. Further, our body's immune system is strengthened, our killer T-cells increase (actually these are the good gals, as they fight cancer and infections), the fats in our blood decrease, blood sugars stabilize.

We are wired for bliss.

So what are the triggers that increase endorphins into our blood steam?

Actually, they are very simple: long-held hugs, kisses in moonlight, stories told to children, chocolate, bike rides along country roads, walks on the snowy mornings, writing poetry, playing the piano, slinging paint at a canvas, riding a merry-go-round, reverence and irreverence, chocolate, a modicum of sass, chocolate, giggles, whoops, chortles, and guffaws, leaps into midair, swimming in a clear, swift river, and, you know it, Baby, chocolate.

The reason Glory Years women are intent on finding the joy-trail is this:

Our very flesh requires it.

It's lunch time: brown bread, cheese, tomatoes, a peanut butter cookie, a diet soda. The Blackberry Tea Club huddles with the food on white sand, a few feet away from the other boaters. We're talking slowly, our laughter subdued. There's a wistfulness about our jokes. We know the trip will be over in an hour. We've been washed clean of civilization, and moving back into the constraints of our real lives carries the weight of sadness.

Leaving Eden always feels like this.

The most turbulent part of the river is still ahead. "Take me home," I murmur, stealing John Denver's song, "country roads . . . to the place where I belong," But I belong here too and don't want to leave. The warm sand feels good on my legs.

We climb into the boats, belt on the life vests, and drift into the current. Melvin is back in his kayak, ready to catch us if we lean too far over the edge of the raft and dump ourselves into the river. We drift for a while, settled, our arms and legs cool in the water. Then we begin to hear the rapids, their murmur soft and low. The sound grows until it is huge, and we have to shout to talk.

The first set of rapids is called Staircase. I've been through Staircase before – sideways. Not sideways sideways, but up-and-down sideways. My brother was rowing through the rapids when the weight in the raft shifted, turned us up on our side, and held. He strong-armed us through the rapids, keeping the tipped boat on track, an amazing feat of strength and oarsmanship.

But I'd rather not do it again, thanks.

We slip through Staircase, careening against boulders. The water is crashing over our heads. We go through flat this time, but it's still a *trip*. We're careening against the rocks, giggling with anticipation, zipping through in the time it takes the human heart to register surprise. But that just whets our appetites for the big water coming next.

The adrenaline is cookin'.

We only have a short way to reorient the raft. We peer, blinkingly, at Slalom, a gnarly (says Melvin) set of rapids. Sam reminds us that these troughs, waves, and keeper holes are dangerous, and we'd best not forget it. He lines us up and shouts, "Buckle down." Sam pulls the raft sideways, sneaking up on the cauldrons, and then plunges us into the center. We lurch one way then another, leaning far out over the edge of the raft, to dig deep, to be strong, to be vital.

My spirit sits up and engages with this river, and I lunge for these rapids, paddling as deeply and strongly as I can. A massive energy surges through my heart and my mind and my body. I am intensely aware of every rock, every wave, the pines, the sage, the curve of the river. I see a summer of buttercups along the shore of the river – not a mass of buttercups, *each buttercup*. The water floods over me, the sound floods over me, light floods over me.

I am nothing but adrenaline and exuberance.

I've been starving my whole life for this.

The rocks and the waves shake us, rock the boats, we shoot from one set of rocks to the next, to the next, and we become Big Water ourselves. My molecules are nothing more than water and air. I am thunderstruck as an explosion of energy envelops me. It is a sensuous energy – energy *physically* in love with all that is – intensity upon intensity, depth unto depth, something larger, more fierce, more joyous than anything I can remember – or imagine.

It comes through the water that drenches me over and over again. It's coming from dry brown dirt, emerald pines, and jade firs, basalt and lava, lichen and lupine, from sage and bitterbrush, from sunlight that darts across the water, from the skin and the heart of the earth, and the sky that cradles us on the planet. I am laughing and crying, sputtering and cooing, shrieking with joy and eating silence alive.

In the middle of one of the biggest, meanest floatable rapids in the world, Miss Priss surfaces. I remember the lessons of poetry. *Duende*, the Spanish poets call it. The Spirit of Earth. Duende is explosive, massive, exuberant, unrepentant, gleeful, sexual energy: tsunami, volcano, lightning strike, earthquake, tornado, hurricane. It is as real as bread, and it binds me to this earth, this sky, this water, these people, and welds me to everything and always.

Our lives are poetry, Miss Priss says. Our experiences are our metaphors. This experience, this trip down a wild and free-flowing river is a metaphor for our midlife passages, our Glory Years, turbulent at times, blessed in others, offering us exuberance that lasts for a moment and the learning that will sculpt the rest of our lives. Like river travel, even when we don't know where we're going, we go there.

We sail on fragile vessels, go headlong into the troughs, paddle our way through air and foam, find the emerald green that is real and pivotal, portage everything we own on wobbly legs, and then smack the river hard when we come through intact. We share an intimacy with beauty, allow the turbulence to scour our spirits clean. Our tears have fed these rivers, kept them salty and earthbound. This is our debt to sorrow and we have paid full up.

This trip down the river is serious play; serious because everything is at stake. I need not to drown. I need to be courageous, to relish these days, to reset my body chemistry on high. It's playful, because anything can happen at anytime and the surprise gives rise to wonder. Life is an extreme sport and we live and work and play within its parameters and directives.

Joy comes from the pit of my belly and from the center of my chest, just behind my breasts, places other than my mind. We usually think of bliss as an ecstatic state. But bliss also might be another thing – it might be the curling around of both spirit and substance, an intimacy with meaning. We luxuriate in the sensibility that our lives are ripe with significance, that our every days are deeper metaphors, that we are fraught with portent.

Signs and portent are harbored in the black basalt, mystery lives in the buttercups and the scent of sage, and enigma inhabits the river water that washes me clean time and time again, physically and spiritually. This sacred sensibility of life is visible, palpable when we engage the most profound part of ourselves in the act of reaching beyond our grasp.

We're no longer stalking joy.

Joy is stalking us.

2

Wearing Our Lives

TUCKED AWAY next to St. Gertrude's, a convent in northern Idaho, a tiny museum houses a happy chaos. Here artifacts tumble against walls bearing witness to the incidents, accidents, tragedies, and miracles that forged pioneer communities from about 1860. Among the treasures are hundred-year-old Dutch ovens, ivory silk dresses with hand-tatted lace, a baby bottle with two nipples (one on either end), and Chinese porcelains from a thousand years away. Nez Percé and Coeur d'Alene artifacts, such as woven baskets and intricate beading, reveal women experienced with an earth we no longer know, artists at play with the natural world.

A short, roundish woman dressed in the dignity of a Benedictine habit rushes toward me. Her garments trail behind her like a storm. Sister Radegunda points to my

T-shirt which reads: "My goal in life is to weigh what my driver's license says I weigh."

"My dear," she asks, patting my hand with stern nunly taps, "have we committed a sin?"

"Yes, Sister." I was on the round side of the scales.

"Have we been fibbing?" Her pats grow more intense.

"Yes, Sister," I pause to consider my moral transgression. "I lied to the great State of Idaho."

"Have we lied a little or a lot?" The pats are insistent.

"A lot, Sister."

"That's okay," she says. "Mine's not right either."

We all lie about our bodies, but they don't lie about us, especially in our middle years. The truth is found in the stretch marks on our bellies and breasts, in the changing shape of our hands and feet, in the quality of the light in our eyes. Our bodies tell the watchful world that we've been a shooting star; that we've lived a three-ring circus; that we're a homemade bed breeding love and warmth; or that we've created a life which is a poetry revealing its depths in the rereading.

We wear our notorious lines and angles as a telling.

Our bodies are our lives made visible: our five-year-old wiggles, our adolescent terrors, the first time we wanted to lick a man clean, what it felt like to put hot tired feet in cool running water. Our bodies manifest the road miles we've run up, the sum total of the pizzas we've slammed into the oven, the number of runny noses we've wiped, and the melodies we've hummed to fill up an empty room. Our bodies express the mountains we've crossed barefooted, the dances we've embraced and the ones we've evaded, and the roses we've nurtured – the ones that would have grown from rocks had we wanted. Our bodies endure our own diseases and dissolution, our own dementias, our own fissures of the soul.

Some nights we sleep the sleep of the wise and the fearless.

Some nights we don't.

Your body is the ground metaphor of your life, the expression of your existence. It is your Bible, your encyclopedia, your life story. Everything that happens to you is stored and reflected in your body. Your body knows, your body tells. The relationship of your self to your body is indivisible, inescapable, unavoidable. In the marriage of flesh and spirit, divorce is impossible.

—GABRIELLE ROTH

Our bodies have born – with such dignity – menarche, sexuality, birthing, parenthood, menopause. These upheavals in our physical selves are forces beyond our reckoning.

What part of us understands, even though we've lived through it, the ramifications of becoming a woman, when all we understood was being a girl? What part of us comprehends what happens when sex takes us over and rides us until we can go no further? What part of us fathoms the birthing that takes us to pleasure and pain at a depth and a breadth no man will ever understand? What part of us knows what loving a toddler, a nine-year-old girl, a twelve-year-old boy, and – *deep sigh here* – what loving an adolescent would do for us – to us? What part of us discerns menopause, beyond the scientific and the medical? What does it mean, what happens to us, when we lose the most essential aspect of womanhood? What part of us figures out how to live with it gracefully, sensibly, and with some measure of power over the last, perhaps, richest years of our lives?

This body knows.

We can trust this flesh.

It's eight in the morning, right after a shower. I'm standing in front of a full-length mirror, inspecting this fifty-two-year-old flesh. If I stand just right, I have giant ripples across my back, three of them in fact. My bare bottom resembles oatmeal to a remarkable degree, as do my thighs. I have a rounded belly and big drooping breasts, although when they are propped up and corralled, I do have a bit of cleavage. My arms are heavy on the top part, my shoulders soft and round.

Perfect.

On the counter in the bathroom, a small goddess rests, a duplicate of the Venus of Willendorf, "the most famous early image of a human, a woman," says Christopher Witcombe. A handmade gift from an old friend. Thirty thousand years ago, holy women looked the way I do now.

I finally have the body of a goddess.

Hunger

These days I'm a fat little health food fanatic careening through contrary appetites for jalapeño potato chips and hot dogs. My cupboard is full of vitamins, herbal teas, cereals with enough fiber to make towels, rubber band-encased packages of brown rice, beans, lentils, pasta, and dried apples. I've developed these little rituals: caffeine in the morning, orange juice midmorning, green tea after lunch, herbal teas in the afternoon. I am prissy about eating meat. Trouble is, I can undo the whole thing on any given afternoon given the unspoken need for something I cannot name. I rove, searching and destroying rum-raisin ice cream, ginger cookies, caramel corn, or anything, anything with butter, anything, anything with sugar.

Women, it seems, are always hungry for the thing they cannot name. How many times have we said to ourselves? *I want something but I don't know what it is.* And then we launched ourselves on a counterterrorist attack, ravaging our refrigerators, our cupboards, our wallets. Our middle-aged bodies are driven by our hungers, the conscious hunger for love and supper, and the unconscious hunger for *something just beyond our knowing*.

But our hungers are more complicated than the search for the perfect little niblet. If that were the case we would have been satisfied by morsels long ago. Certainly, we've gone through enough of them. Our hungers are deep and persistent. Our hungers are telling us a truth, one that is just on the tip of our tongues.

Our bodies in our Glory Years hunger for righteous food. Righteous food puts iron in our blood, steel in our backbone, and fire in our eyes. Righteous food is dark chocolate, red wine, moonlight, and the men who make us yearn for them. It is fried chicken, potato salad, thick slices of tomatoes, watermelon – the food of family. It is lemonade and sugar cookies served in glossy gardens, dazed with columbine and wisteria, and the generous laughter of friends. It is shimmering pasta, black mushrooms, garlic, and ginger served next to slow-moving rivers on soil not our own.

We are starved for mashed potatoes and gravy and Emily Dickinson.

We are starved for milk and honey and Aretha Franklin.

We are starved for bread and butter and Georgia O'Keeffe.

We are hungry for what is whole, what is wholesome, what is holy. Our bodies know, in our viscera, how it feels to teach a child to read or to heal an open wound. We are eager to give something substantial to our community, perhaps money, because the lack of money may be the only thing standing between a problem and its solution. We are ravenous for play that connects us to a community of players, for art that connects us to a community of artists. What we are voracious for is this: the wealth and weight of family, the dignity of learning, the safety of community, the mystery of the open road, the essence of wonder.

Like many other women, I've been rail-thin *and* I've expanded my boundaries about as far as they will go. My extra weight might be the product of a loopy metabolism, a diabolical obsession with chocolate, an inordinate addiction to cherry pie and a long sit-down, or:

Maybe I needed a thicker skin to protect me from the pain in my life.

Maybe my weight is a brace against life, an excuse to be a nonparticipant.

Maybe my weight is a side effect of my life.

An outcome.

Bodies in Motion

When my body grew too dense and too wide for my own comfort, it was, I think, because I lost touch with the pleasure of moving. Life is so complex and unforgiving at times, and the only things that soothe are stillness, quietness, and a little something sweet. I'm not the only woman in the world who has retreated to the comfort of a televised hour with Oprah and lemon creams.

When we settle in, *we settle in.*

The last time I went to the gym, I promised myself, after an hour and a half of being pummeled by an old Bee Gees tune in a hundred-degree wooden box shared with forty cantankerous women, that I'd never do another exercise that left me in the back row, drenched in sweat, embarrassed, or undignified. This fifty-year-old body bristles at aerobics with its imposed regimens. But as I watched women who were punishing themselves on StairMasters for the crime of aging, for growing softer and wider, I knew I needed a sweeter way to move.

Fortunately, I found an old girl who knew exactly what I needed – my own old girl. The girl had aged, but she still resided in this flesh. She was the one who still knew how to hop, skip, and leap through airy nothing, to walk in dangerous places, and run with the wind, and dance and dance and dance.

She knew her own ability to move, knew natural rhythms and deep contentments, knew what was safe and what was not. The breath, the heartbeat, the reach of muscle, what felt fine, what caused pain – these were her parameters. She was constructed for pleasure, not for speed, for movement that soothed, calmed, invigorated, rejoiced – exercise that was playful and private.

My own body taught me to dance again, to stroll along rivers, to stride across hills, to stretch with the ancient rhythms of yoga, to swim deeply and profoundly in moving waters. I danced to music I loved: vintage Beatles songs; thunderous classics by lusty venerable Russians; Bonnie Raitt and Bette Midler, women with a few road miles on their bodies as well. One morning, I hit the edge of a canyon just at dawn, listening to Wynona wail "Jesus in the Sky." Another night I danced to the ancient rhythms and unfamiliar melodies of Hildegard of Bingen – with only the moon for company. "Sweat your prayers," Gabrielle Roth says.

I remembered the moves I had lost as a child: a butterfly ballet that had me flitting from one flower to another (a ludicrous moment that had me roaring with laughter); a ships-at-sea-tossed-in-a-raging-storm tango; the hula I did with a flower tucked behind my ear; the Las Vegas showgirl strut I did when I was nine and dressed in my mother's black slip. Flying hops, rampaging skips, Irish jigs that sent butt jiggling, breasts headed every which way. It helped to laugh – early and often. At home, the draperies shut tight, sometimes naked, always barefoot, I recovered the playfulness of movement.

I stretched into yoga, practicing with tapes produced by two round-bodied women whose flesh was as dense and thick as my own. What in the beginning seemed deadly dull, took on meaning as spirit and flesh both came alive under those benign moves. The flesh responds to gentleness, a repose beyond consciousness.

I swam, relearning to trust the water, our birth fluid, learning to float in living waters – rivers and small pools – in the only space that makes us feel like flying between heaven and earth.

Growing stronger, more graceful adds a substantial measure of joy to my days. Getting fitter, a little thinner was a byproduct of pleasure, not the goal. I'll never go back to the strength of my twenty-year-old body. That's all right. Children love to snuggle against these breasts, and babies find a purchase on these hips – as do my men.

When I move my body, my heart opens. I'm inclined to walk three miles barefoot through cool, wet grass on a hot day, or put on gypsy music and dance until my head spins, or move into the yoga stretches that take the body just past infinity.

Sensitivity

It's hard for me to get the kids to bed on time, so it's late when my nephew, Scottie, is finally in his crib and my niece, Mackenzie, is in her pink flannel jams, beginning to settle. Scott is energetic as toddlers are, so getting him to bed, an hour-and-a-half endeavor, requires persistence, creativity, persistence, cajoling, persistence, focus.

Did I mention persistence?

Mackenzie and I have just settled into our story time. "Tell me a for-reals story," she says. She likes the old stories of the farm, the time her dad got his poor little toes pecked by chickens. These giggles, this snuggle time are what aunts live for.

And then, in the middle of a sentence, I get up and walk into Scottie's room with no apparent reason to do so. But my body gets me there just as this beloved boy is about to climb over the railing of his crib. I hadn't latched one side of the railing correctly and he'd found an escape.

I still shudder.

I believe this is a universal experience with Glory Years women: our physical bodies guiding our steps rather than our minds. We might rub a place on our skin unconsciously, comforting and healing, before we spot the bruise or remember how we got it. How many times has this happened? And we do that for our children and our men as well. Our bodies are increasingly sensitive to things our minds cannot know.

We enter a room full of people and *physically* feel their depressions and anxieties – even when they've hidden those feelings under the guise of good humor and a stiff drink or two. It may have taken us a decade or two to realize that those feelings were not our own, that we were sensing what other people were feeling. These status reports are the basis of our compassion and our torment. Our minds absorb and digest a thousand details, and our bodies process them into a knowing. This involuntary process may come from our internal mechanism for making sure people are all right, the thing women have been doing since the advent of time.

We grow more sensitive by the day. Medications may seem several times stronger than when we took them last. Caffeine becomes as potent as adrenaline. Salt and sugar act like corporate raiders on the lookout for plunder. The speed of wine is fast and getting faster. Remember when we could stay up all night? Fueled by greasy nachos and pitchers of cheap beer?

Can we do it now? Do we even want to?

When we retreat to a hot fudge sundae or a basket of French fries, the result feels like nuclear meltdown. We feel viscerally what is good for us and what is not, where harm resides and where health abounds. Our physical intuition, so often considered flaky or insubstantial, turns out to be as trustworthy as salt.

Once in a while, I go on press trips. This one was in South Dakota during the spring of 2000. South Dakota is a great, gracious space – prairie with an eternity of green, winds that come from nowhere and blow through like a full-throttle freight train headed east, a generous people who create the glorious and the loopy straight out of nothing. The beloved Rushmore dazzles both spirit and substance. Abe made me cry – again. A few years ago, in Washington, D.C., I walked up the steps into the Lincoln Memorial and wept where I stood.

The Badlands and Black Hills are geologies like no other. The spires in the Badlands come and go as they will; it is a landscape that is not entirely solid. What looks like rock isn't. It's an amalgam of ash, clay, and sand, and the natural sculptures drift and dance with the wind and the rain. Striations of blood, gold, bronze held against a turquoise sky would tell you their stories if they could sit still long enough.

And the Black Hills seem like Hobbit mountains, smaller by four thousand feet than the peaks of my own Idaho. The vistas hold mesmeric properties: the dark and lumbering buffalo, the prairie dogs who living in social systems more loving than our own, and wild donkeys who will sneak donuts from your hand.

Unlikely things happen here.

A young, brilliant Lakota woman told me that the Black Hills are sacred, taken from her people by the lust for Black Hills gold. Later, while walking through the Black Hills near Crazy Horse (a mountain is being made into an in-the-round sculpture of Crazy Horse, the revered Lakota warrior), I knelt down and touched the mica-rich dirt, softened by sand and ash. The black soil was luminous. Light in these mountains comes from within.

She also suggested that I visit a store in Rapid City called Prairie Edge, a habitat for museum quality art and reproductions of Indian artifacts. There, sculptures of women resonant with story; beaded leathers tell me not of a savage culture but one of artisans. A huge buffalo hide was draped over a piece of furniture. The hair on the hide was six inches deep, soft as down. I wanted to throw myself on the hide and stay there, nose down, for the rest of my life. I was adamantly in love. I wanted to take it home, but its ten-thousand-dollar price tag was a deterrent. Instead, I touched it again and again so I would never forget what that animal felt like, and that its life spirit would reside within me.

No wonder these hills, these animals are so treasured by the Lakota.

The next day we drove through Custer State Park, and I saw the buffalo. A herd of cows and red calves moved slowly across the highway, and later, against a vibrant green hill, stood a single magnificent black bull. Nobility on the hoof, a majestic masculinity.

We stopped for lunch at a lodge made of dark logs, surrounded by a downed tree and a plethora of spring flowers. We were served buffalo stew in a bread bowl, the sauce rich with potatoes and carrots. It was delicious, but I've been a vegetarian for a long time, and the stew was a real stretch for me. I was nervous about eating it, *something told me not to eat it,* but it seemed more trouble than it was worth to make a fuss. Besides, it was cold in April in the mountains, and the stew was warm.

I ate it. And threw up on the bus not two hours later. No sleep, a wobbly bus ride on a curvy road, a body and a soul that could not, would not accept buffalo flesh – I didn't stand a chance. I should have heeded that voice.

That voice.

What is good and what is bad for human beings is most pronounced in us. Glory Years women feel first the cracks in the eggshell of family, community, and society, places where infection or spoil can creep in, broken places that invite harm.

We are the indicator species.

Menopause

Technically, I went through menopause in about an hour and a half. At forty-two, my uterus and my ovaries were removed. I had fibroids as big as a four-month-old fetus, so there went the uterus. My ovaries were taken because too many people on both sides of my family have had cancer, particularly my mother and grandmother.

The surgery and the physical recovery were not difficult. I'd hoped the pathway through estrogen would be easier. Spiritually, emotionally, it was arduous.

The unknown is daunting. My body shuddered and wept

when major parts went missing. There was a keening in my soul so intense, it must have reverberated across the dry hills of my homeland, an echoing sadness, a dense and sustained despair. The wounded animal appeared, curled around itself, holding the sliced-open belly, cradling the pain. I was only capable of silence and stillness. The calm rationality of science and medicine – the cancer scare, the growing fibroids, the assurances of the ease of the new estrogens – had no bearing on this grief.

This body would have none of it.

After the hysterectomy, I gobbled down estrogen like it was candy. The night sweats, the overwhelming feelings of massive fatigue and vulnerability – who would do such a thing to this body? the animal wanted to know – were physical symptoms that masked a greater pain. I was depressed to a degree I had not thought possible.

I went to my doctor, my trusted surgeon, who, nonetheless, had never lived through *this*. Because of the breast cancer history in my family, he was worried about giving me more estrogen. He was walking away from me when I asked for more estrogen. "No, no," he said. "I don't think you need more estrogen, I think you are depressed and in need of counseling."

"All right," I said. "I'm a mess. I'll go."

That stopped him in his shoelaces and he turned back around, flapping his white coat and his stethoscope against his body. He stared at me. "You're not in denial. Oh, my God! Maybe you do need more estrogen."

I decided to go to counseling instead of increasing the estrogen, although it was a tough go. The reason for the depression: I had not had children, probably the only thing I truly wanted in life. *I grieved.*

My doctor and I entered a six-year tussle with estrogen, progesterone, patches of varying dosages, herbs. I felt as if there were a stranger in my body, as close to a diagnosis of lunacy as there is. But I didn't feel crazy, I felt *crazed.* I gained forty pounds in a heartbeat, increased my blood pressure, and took on water like a sinking ship. But I knew my body needed the estrogen for a while, so I went with it.

And then one morning, three or four years into the process, I knew I needed less. It took two years of slowly decreasing the estrogen, lower and lower doses, until it was a very small step to stop entirely. And so I did.

I went a little nuts. The same week, I attended a writing camp in the eastern Oregon and submitted the first draft, of my first chapter, of my first novel to a New York editor. (Don't *ever* do this, particularly your first week off estrogen.) He tried to be kind, God bless him, but he was trying to snow me, trying to tell me what the novel was about, tried to pigeonhole it into a genre, which told me he hadn't read it. The trouble was this: I hadn't engaged him enough in the first page or two for him to read the rest of the material.

I had profoundly failed in my task. I sat on a log around the campfire and cried for four solid days, a horror for the other writers who knew it could have been any one of them. (The editor was at least kind to me. He told an attorney at the camp that the poor man wasn't a writer, would never be a writer, and to never think about it again. Ever.)

I came home in a rash of urgency, wanting to quit writing. I went to my writing group and told them I was going to quit and go teach daycare because little kids liked my stories. "I'll shoot you first," the physician-novelist said. And his humor was the slap on the rear that let me inhale a little fresh air. A birth breath.

Still, this post-estrogen woman was not entirely sane.

But then things got a little easier, and a little better. I calmed down and gained a little distance, a little clarity.

While I was at that writers' camp, I rode a gondola to the top of 8,200-foot Mount Howard and took pictures, one snap after the next, of eight glorious peaks capped with snow in July. The pictures came back and I glued them, in the series that they were taken, to my writing desk. I have a broad panorama of those exquisite mountains on a day when the sky was filled with clouds and the tundra was alive with microscopically small flowers. Perspective is everything, the clouds and the mountains say to me: *Look to the long view.*

The long view applied to menopause as well.

When I stopped the estrogen, the stranger left my physical self. The animal body quit grieving and healed entirely. In fact, she is a bit frisky now, very free, and subject to growing fits of exuberance and laughter. My sense of my physical self is back. I feel normal, a blessed thing.

The thing is this: every woman's pathway through menopause is so profoundly different from any other. *Studies say* is the old saw, the studies that look at hundreds of thousands of females (that's what they call us in the studies) and miss the thready lives of individual women. Judy says that when estrogen came back into her body, she felt like she was welcoming her old self back. Marianne started taking Premarin twelve years ago, and it worked perfectly, still works perfectly. Mary is beginning to have a few hot flashes. Marty may feel not much at all; she is particularly fit and active and may not even notice the changes until they have happened. Angie was drenched in debilitating night sweats, heart palpitations, and mood swings that would startle Lucrezia Borgia. Julie's periods are two months or two years apart, have been so since she was a teenager. If she feels well, she might not know for four years. What studies account for these extremes?

When I worked at a medical center, I prepared media, such as slides or handouts for physician's presentations. We were in a documentation fervor; source and study attribution had to be in plain view, in large enough letters to be seen from the back of the room.

When I asked a presenter, whose talk was on estrogen

replacement therapy, where the documentation was for her statements, she said there wasn't any. Studies were in progress . . . "Are doctors all over the country prescribing estrogen to millions of women without knowing whether it's safe or not?" I was outraged. She shrugged.

There were a few voices crying in the wilderness. A beloved, local oncologist suggested that the rise in breast cancer paralleled the rise in long-term estrogen use and there might be a connection.

It turned out he was on to something. And as the truth about estrogen replacement therapy surfaced, I felt betrayed by systems that were meant to protect our hearts, our bones, our memories.

So what do we do?

Bring the power home, Baby. Learn everything there is to learn. Trust your own sweet flesh. Hot flashes and all.

The question that turned out to be essential was this: Did I trust Mother Nature's design and pattern, Her pathway for women? That the cessation of estrogen was a right and good thing, when it came at a right and good time, and that this woman's body would know when it needed less estrogen and more of something else?

But I truly needed the estrogen for a while. I was only forty-two when I had my hysterectomy. But there came a time when this body's need for estrogen was not so intense, not so persistent. And I trusted that. Other women must watch their bones. Their memories. Their over-heated bodies.

The thing is this: we have to figure it out for ourselves. One woman's pathway is another woman's maze. Menopause is so real, so troubling, so much work, there must be a physical and spiritual reward for enduring it.

There is. Dr. Joan Borysenko, a psychoimmunologist turned wise woman, writes in *A Woman's Book of Life* that menopause may be a birth. Not a rebirth, a birth. The long dark tunnel we need to go through to meet our most essential and powerful selves. Dr. Joan says that when estrogen decreases, the pituitary kicks in, and two very powerful hormones are released, the hormones of outspokenness and courage. Dr. Joan calls this phase of life "the Guardian," the woman who goes to battle for the right things in the right way and at the right time, the older woman who is fierce and fine and free.

I believe that Glory Years women are birthing their next beautiful selves, women with intense compassion and fire in the soul, women with a massive will to express whatever truth there is, women fueled with the molecules of courage born up on the wings of experience.

We have to get past the thought that menopause is an illness that needs to be treated or a step toward death that needs to be avoided or postponed.

We can perceive menopause as a stepping stone, a way

marker along our path. It is the ending of one phase of our lives, but it is also the beginning of the next. Some women find the empty nest a horror, but others will find that as their primary task of raising children is finishing, another is beginning – the unfolding of their most brilliant, most powerful selves.

After menopause, there is a raw energy or a clarity that is new to us. We need more rest and sex (the nicest of surprises), long swims in cool water (still the best and most reliable treatment for hot flashes). We need walks everywhere, hungry as we are for the way the world looks, close up, right now.

We grow contemplative and creative, adamant that we are to be spiritually and intellectually mature as well. Always there is the search for truth, although now we find most of the news is good, grounded as we are in a long compassion for ourselves and for other people, acquainted as we are with human frailty and human hope.

Our bodies are quieter now, not given to moon swings or days when we increase a dress size because it is hot or we've eaten too much salt. It is great to not be nauseated and befuddled two days a month. It is glorious to know what we feel is what we feel. When we are angry, we are angry. When we are desperate, the desperation is the result of an interaction with life, not an interaction of hormones. When we are sad, we do not have to apologize or explain or deny. We don't have to check the calendar to see if we are suffering from PMS. When we are fussy or opinionated or tempestuous, that's what we are. Our vitality, our will, our intellect, and our feelings are as real as bread, as useful as money.

> The moon hung full over the hills. Unhurried by the day's first light, she reveled in her fullness. I went outside to sit in contemplation of her, and we faced each other in utter equanimity: She who had pulled the tides of my inner sea for 450-some months, powerfully, capriciously, violently, now had relaxed her hold on me and left my waters calm as a lagoon after a tropical storm. Emptied, I sat there in the twig-brushing breeze and savored the quiet aliveness that had come to me at last.
>
> —GAIL SHEEHY

If we can live through menopause, we can live for anything.

Sensuality

Most cities have small, eclectic neighborhoods, where artists, writers, gardeners, and athletes gather, where coffee shops, used-book stores, and antique galleries collect browsers, where grand old trees drop golden leaves into the November streets. In my hometown, Boise, this older neighborhood is Hyde Park. There is a white clapboard church, one with windows that open to the street and the night air. Late on a Friday night, people gather, wearing primal colors, who've caught the fever of rhythm: drummers and dancers and poets.

The Middle-Eastern dancers appear first. Draped in purple and black veils, bangles and sequins, two women emerge from the shadows. The first woman, mysterious in black, is a little heavy: a soft, rolled belly, large breasts, and hips that round out from her waist. For a few minutes, a murmur of judgment rises against her, but she's used to that and patiently begins to woo us. She fills the room with a lyrical, languid sensuality. Her womanly roundedness turns softness into a celebration.

Shrouded in sapphire veils, the next woman is stunningly fit. The muscle in her diaphragm writhes, giving the word undulation a physical definition. I watch the men in the room — they are going to need oxygen soon.

For the last dance, the two women invite people from the audience to join them. Sophia rises from the floor. She's in her late forties, dressed in a black leotard and a sarong she knots at her waist. She too is round, losing her waist to children and the responsibilities of middle age. But she enters the dance with abandon, her hips joyously, in sync with the wild cadences that fill the room. The quality of the light and the air changes. The three women twirl and flow, trailing indigo, sapphire, and scarlet veils, throwing sparks a hundred feet. As they slip from the room, the man at the microphone proudly announces this: all three women are grandmothers.

In these years, we are no longer sexy; *we are sex*. We are as luscious as night-blooming flowers, sweet as caramel, soft as butter. We are as decadent as a two-hundred-dollar bottle of wine, as rare, as rich, as sweet, as seductive. We are as mysterious as moonstones and tiger's eyes, stones with depth and movement.

Sex, for us, is not so much about how we look, or how our men look, or about our mastered techniques which are useless in the face of love anyway. Sex now is about connection, communion, bonding, an intimate knowing. It is love play with the man who is mirror to us. It is the gentle teasing and the being teased, holding and the withholding, the playfulness that catches our hearts first, then pulls the rest of our beleaguered, then eager, selves along.

As it turns out, just about everything becomes sensual, a succulent response to life: slow jazz, deep purple cherries, fireflies over a meandering river, track meets and ballets – those beautiful bodies – Grand Marnier, the laughter of children, Neruda's poems, bare feet in cool water. It can all unhinge us, leave us open and ready for whatever comes next. We hold nothing back. These are wonderful aphrodisiacs: safety, playfulness, and the will to love well, an open vital response to life. We wrap sex in dignity.

Our bodies know that sex is more than skin-deep. Our

fireworks have been replaced by the deeper rhythms of the seas and the stars. Sex comes from the inside out, our minds, our hearts, our wombs, our vaginas are the birthplace of ardor. We've lost our self-consciousness; our bodies know what they are to be about. It is the releasing, opening, responding, surrendering, not only to our men, but to ourselves, to our deep internal organs. We are luscious as blackberries, soft as butter. Our deep interior spaces have provided such sweetness for our men, nurturing and sustaining their lives with our presence.

When we share our most vulnerable, sacred, beautiful bodies, something more than the physical is touched. We know why sex is so serious now, why love bequeaths life, and why the lack of it leaves us raw and vulnerable, takes away our sense of ourselves. A single kiss can change the course of a life. Or a long look. Something of the experience, good or bad, remains in our flesh, in our memory for as long as we breathe. So we are immensely careful with whom we share our flesh, our souls. The fireworks last but a few minutes, but the conflagrations, combustions, contingencies, and consequences of sex ripple over generations, over communities.

"I come from thirty miles deep," wrote poet Rachel Ward. We are aroused from the inside out. Those deep interior organs have the feel of the tides about them. Love rides us in waves, waves that come from deep inside us. We delight in passion, playfulness, a wicked imagination, a laughter that comes from our core, a stunning freedom that we might have, somehow, failed to mention to our younger sisters or to the men who passed us by.

This is the best interior giggle.

Ever.

The Wild Radish is a merry pairing of field and barn: straw pasted to the stucco walls, silk foliage winding around the whitewashed posts that hold the roof up. It is a bit of whimsy, a restaurant flourishing inside four country walls.

Late night in Ketchum, Gwynne, Juanita, and I stop there to have dinner after a long drive, after a long week. We are subdued by road weariness, the exhaustion of our bodies evident in our faces.

The next table over are three other women, blonde and substantial, not quite a generation younger. They fill up the small room with raucous laughter, there to celebrate Jasmine's fortieth birthday. Jasmine's blond hair is pulled back from her face. She wears heavy gold loop earrings and the understated clothing of women with a history of money. Obviously, they've hit two or three other restaurants to nibble and tipple. They are at the Wild Radish to share a "Mousse in a Bag" and a bottle of champagne. Chocolate and bubbly.

Jasmine occasionally shouts, "No. No! I'm really, really only thirty." Adrienne is pulling back the skin on her face with her hands and sputtering, "If only I could drape this stuff over my ears." Jessie, plumper than the other two, tugs at her breasts and yells, "Oh, this body! Oh, this body!" They are screaming with laughter.

Impossible to ignore, they strike up conversations with people at tables near them. We laugh with them gingerly, for we are too tired for such shenanigans. But when we get up to leave, we go to their table to shake Jasmine's hand, wish her a happy birthday and more, safe passage. Because each of us had gone screaming through that tumultuous birthday, and know the danger and the glory that awaits her.

We wished we knew then what we know now: That life gets better, that it gets harder; that we get wiser and more forgetful in equal measure; that we find life funnier and more poignant; that our power increases as does our frustration; that we do not give up sex, that we do not give up play, that our bodies grow softer, our minds more astute, our hearts grow bigger as well, that our sweet, sacred flesh takes on a contrary life of its own and that we are along for the ride.

No one explained to us that the wrinkles meant our skin grew larger than our bodies because we needed the extra room just to get comfortable. That our whitening hair forms an aura that radiates and attracts light. That our forgetfulness signals preoccupation with larger ideas, more powerful concerns. Or that "a generosity of spirit and a liveliness of intellect" (a line borrowed from Isabelle Allende) draws men to us both in mysterious and complex ways, interest that is sustained over time.

Our eyes see at odd moments glory,
the worth of our children, the vulnerability of our men.
We see mystery in the veins of a lettuce leaf and magic
in the upwelling of tulips in February
when it is still cold and dark.
We weep with the wild winds.

Our ears hear the moments of stillness in our homes
when our children are suddenly up to something.
We hear differences:
the difference in the sounds of one season
evolving into another;
the difference between one breath and the next
when the heart has changed direction;
the difference in the sigh of an adolescent
who is sulking or one in real pain.

Our lips form kisses, prayers, poems, promises,
rages, and opinions,
frame our songs and screams, wails, and whispers.
We taste peaches and sweet wine, the salt of skin,
nubs of pencils.

Our breasts host a suckling and a pleasure,
an immeasurable sensitivity,
a magnet for men who invigorate us,
a snuggling place for children who need a home base.
Nothing any where, at any time, in any way, is any softer.
These breasts are pillows for the soul.

Our hands steady our men, nourish our children,
wild creatures that they are.
These fingers and palms
clean, comfort, cherish,
incite, excite, sustain,
command, create, correct,
heal, help,
and love and love and love.

Our bellies host a place of sturdy knowing,
a receptivity and sensitivity,
a center for truth when it finally surfaces.
Truth registers there, resonates there, resides there.
As do our intuitions.

Our wombs are slowly drying,
but life is still birthed there, defined now as
generosity and grace, fire and will, silence and space.
These days we birth other things.
We birth well-being, wisdom, wistfulness.
Our vaginas, bless them, our dark, deep pink roses,
still call our men and provide a luscious nest for them.

Our feet walk unlikely paths, across warm sand,
over stone mountains, wade through high water
and trail through the gardens of our own making.

The truth is this:
at this age, we are regal, matriarchal, majestic, and sacred.
Each of us is more than merely beautiful.
Our bodies are worthy of the tenderest of touches,
worthy of emerald days, amethyst dusks, and ruby dawns,
worthy of rambles in beautiful places,
worthy of white silk,
worthy of dark chocolate,
worthy of pearls and violets,
worthy of belly laughs, worthy of cries in the night,
worthy of the long slow dance.

3

Tenderness in Every Direction

TANYA, MY COUSIN, and I talk far into the California night, blinking with tired eyelids, sipping tea from porcelain teacups and their mismatched saucers, about family, children, work, the multiple directions of our lives are taking; whether our summer reads were mind candy or crotch novels. Santa Cruz in August.

The next morning the fog burns off the ocean by noon. The air is gathering warmth and feels luscious against my skin, accustomed to harsh desert air. Tanya is finishing tasks required to teach a new semester, so I opt to spend Sunday afternoon on the beach.

As we round the black cypress sculpted against white stone cliffs overlooking the surfers bobbing on the waves, I'm mesmerized – the middle-years surfers along the road strip down to their barest nothings as they climb into or out of their gear. They shed T-shirts, baggy shorts, teeny briefs with abandon. I loved surfers when I was a teenager watching beach movies, and I love them now. I sneak tiny looks, giggle like a fourteen year old. The old joy juice still propels.

Plopping down on my towel, I stretch out beside a volume of mind candy, maybe a crotch novel, but the book lies unopened in the sand. A sun-bleached five year old and his golden retriever scamper through the waves. Their play turns droplets of sea water into tiny prisms.

Staring at sea, sky, sand is enough.

Drifting in and out of reverie, I notice that people on the beach are staring at me.

All of them.

That's a bit unnerving.

So I look the other direction. It's no different. These people also hold the same unblinking stares, compounded by a shake of the head.

Unbelievable, the nods indicate.

I am an Idaho woman, but does it show? Were these faded blue shorts and mismatched shirt a clue? My ten-year-old sandals?

Parents stroll in front of me, turning their children's heads toward the sea.

Oh, boy.

The perplexing combo of being stared at and patently ignored continues for some time. I look at the waves, hoping my ears aren't red, and then peek down the beach. They are still looking at me, igniting my fires of self-consciousness in a big way.

Trying to catch a glimpse of the people on the beach is hard to do if you can't turn your head. My eyes furtively glance left to right; my head bobs up and down. I look like a weasel. People are as rapt as ever.

Then I hear a whisper of skin against sand. I turn around just enough to see two pairs of feet.

Twitterpated feet.

Not a body length behind me, a dark-headed man with beautiful haunches and a honey-haired girl are mating silently as snails.

I bury my eyes in my right hand. Laughter topples me over in the sand, and I can't get up. The people closest to me are in on the joke: a couple completes the grand act of love not three feet away from an utterly oblivious middle-aged woman, one in Idaho clothes and ten-year-old sandals. In a few seconds, we are snorting with laughter, utterly losing any sense of composure. The jig is up. The couple readjusts clothing, grabs their towels and Pepsi cans and strolls away, sighing, arm in arm.

Just when you think you're at the center of your own universe, you aren't.

A few daydreams later, I notice a tiny black potbellied pig a ways down the beach. The little guy is pummeling the sand, his tiny legs sending up small flares. He looks like he's running in slow motion, because he is working so hard to gain so little distance.

He seems to be running toward me.

He is.

Stopping less than a foot in front of me, he looks up at me with the small black eyes of love. Snort. The little pig threatens a snuggle.

"Hi, sweetheart." I nuzzle his sweet face.

The pig leans into me with an amorous cooing. Out of two hundred or so people on this small white beach, the pig chooses me to harbor a quick affection.

His owners, dressed in the exuberance of the late 1960s, walk up to me in a few minutes. They tell me that Oscar picks up women on the beach, that their itty-bitty pig has an unfailing radar for women who will love him back. For fifteen or twenty minutes, I scratch his ears, his belly, tenderly touch his face, kiss the top of his head. I wrap my arms around him and cuddle him.

Contentment oozes over him, like hot fudge on vanilla ice cream. Finally, his owners lure him away with blackberries.

Love is playing with me.

I am as befuddled by love as anything else in all of life. When my therapist asked me what I would like to have written on my tombstone, I had a quick answer: *She loved well, but not at all wisely.*

Bless her, my counselor worked so hard to achieve a professional demeanor with me, but this time she dissolved into laughter. I was in my early forties at the time, with a string of misbegotten loves and amorous miswhacks. If people had told me how romantic love would evolve in my life, I would have shot them.

Apparently love, though, does not leave us alone. Love wraps itself around me and guides these words and shapes the experiences of my life. Love plays with me sometimes, tangling around my need and self-consciousness, showing up at unexpected moments, leaving footprints I decipher only after the fact. The most any of us understand is a tiny slice of a 360-degree circle of love, just a degree or two. Maybe three.

If we are very, very lucky.

The First Degree

In the mountains of central Idaho, the sunset side of the Rockies, my brother and his family have a small cabin on a promontory that overlooks Cascade Lake. We're there for the weekend. Saturday night Mackenzie, my niece, and Scott, my nephew, and I played "Idiot," a card game that left us screaming in triumph or disaster, ate blackberry cobbler and vanilla ice cream with the family, and then slept with the stars not far from our heads.

Sunday morning, after coffee with its steaming curlicues and a little time for gratitude, I am meandering with the kids down a path to the lake, a blue dazzler. It's August and too dry, but perfect otherwise. The ponderosa and yellow pine creak softly; the aspen flutter their silvered leaves whether or not there is a breeze. Widget, more formally known as Scottie, is seven years old, and his sister, Miss Mackenzie, is eleven going on twenty-five. She is the old soul in the family, the poet, the actress and the dancer, the child with the wicked sense of humor. For Christmas this year, she wore a tiny coonskin cap – on her big toe. Her long blond hair is in its usual thick braid and she moves with fluidity and intention through a stand of blue spruce. Widget is endlessly curious, the child who could say pachy-cephalosaurus on his second birthday. He is running his hand over the branches of sage brush, releasing the scent. Every inch of ground for him is loaded with enchantment. Mackenzie is staring at the sky, quiet and internal, listen-ing to larger rhythms. Nature is teaching us, one dragonfly, one chipmunk, one startled jay at a time, to love Her. The air settles us into a rightful place.

After lunch we pack up for the drive back to Boise. Miss Mackenzie, Widget, and I snuggle into the back seat of the Bronco. I'm in the middle. The road before us is twisty and narrow so the kids opt for sleep. They both lean into my soft flesh and their touch opens channels of energy between us. I can literally feel their love penetrating my body, the way water enters a sponge. Apparently, love is a force of its own devising. It comes in waves and flows through all three of us, back and forth and through. Each wave more poignant than the last.

Love must be like a photon, both a particle and a wave, both a thing and an energy; the thing from which everything beautiful or useful appears, and the energy from which everything worthy arises.

Rabbi George said this: "Our children teach us about love, even when we have forgotten."

The Second Degree

When I fall into love, I want to cook.

Lasagna.

I relish the peeling of roasted garlic, the little soft bodies emerging from their skins, blanching spinach, lacing it with onions, butter, and balsamic vinegar, then folding fresh basil and pine nuts into the ricotta, at last settling crimini into the olive oil and lemon and snuggling the fennel inside. These tasks celebrate the sensual and become a gift to the man I love. I touch his face with hands still redolent of the essential oils of lemon and basil.

My man is light, something within him is incandescent. At times I think I can see his essential soul, like the essential oils of lemon or basil – gifts of the interior, aromatic with meaning and depth. Most of the time, though, his eyes betray a loneliness, even for a man embroiled in the deepest needs of many people. We have our own distances as well. Sometimes my shyness creates distance; sometimes his preoccupations do. The merlot loosens harried responsibility from his grip. The lasagna is a living, earthy food, and the sustenance nourishes our fragile cells. We eat greens from someone's garden and hearty bread, smeared with butter. His shoulders relax, and the stories of the day emerge.

Why is it that passion and compassion are so inextricably bound?

We lose our distances. This we know how to do. I slow down enough to listen for his heartbeat and for his breath, to touch and be touched. This man is an embodiment of tenderness, timelessness, imagination: the most sensual, sexual gifts. My mind forgets to think. We become a tangle of illuminated arms and legs, eyes closed and hearts open, a combustion of traveling kisses and fingertips laced with fire. I am at the mercy of warrior hands, healer hands, and the incorrigible, merry male. Lovemaking, in this time and in this place, resembles the waves of the ocean as our bodies expand and contract. This odd beauty takes us to the end of desire, the long, entwining embrace, the soul contract of lovers.

Love makes me real as salt.

The Third Degree

Our local coffee shop, The Flying M, is a rich old haunt. The walls are painted India pink and turquoise in spirals, deep red with underlying textures. Fifties couches, round oak tables, overstuffed chairs – none of which match – are scattered through the room. Outside the February fog leans against the store front windows, already steamy from the espresso machine.

We meet Friday mornings, five writers, Diane, Mary, Judy, Marsha, and I. We come because we need to. It's the place where we share our work at times, but most often we offer evidence of progress: completed projects, letters written to editors, contacts made. If we work alone too much, we are answerable to no one. This makes us accountable and productive.

This week The Flying M is hosting a valentine art show, a charity event raising money for AIDS education. We wander through the exhibition, an irreverent demonstration of the whole spectrum of love, the good to the inexplicable. A small bed, the size of my palm, is embraced by tiny roses, an arbor for a small poem, but the poem takes a wicked turn. On another shelf, a neon sign blazes a forlorn yearning, brash and keening.

And in an out-of-the-way corner, we find a tiny photograph, no more than two inches in any direction, framed in the dignity of black. I am taken aback, not expecting to see what I think I am seeing.

It is a vagina.

Unabashedly open.

In the shape of a perfect valentine heart.

I'd always wondered where that shape had come from, archetypal shape that it is. Obviously, the valentine heart does not resemble the human heart – our hearts are tilted ovals. But the thought that leaves me thunderstruck is this: Our most intimate, sacred place, the birthing place of our children, the holy grail our men seek and seek and seek, is the ardent symbol of love.

Our physical identity is love.

Only 357 Degrees of Love to Go

Glory Years women no longer use love as a proper noun. We are more likely to use it as an active verb. *Love* is a fantasy for young women with visions of young males with perfect abs, voluminous white dresses with jealous attending friends, a little later, bubbling babies. I used to think that love should be for a certain rather predictable man, for the two children I cherish, for my family and friends, that if any of those loves were diminished, I was diminished as well.

A little bit of that is true.

But as I grew into my Glory Years, something insidious crept into my subconscious. I subscribed to the notion depicted in our homogenized, mall-strewn, media-blasted culture that middle-aged women's love was trivial and feeble, without passion or intention, that it was manageable and marginalized, that we were hormonally imbalanced, spendy, whiny empty nesters or the odd aunt who brought the olives for Christmas dinner.

The part that is massively wrong-headed and debilitating is the notion that our Glory Years' love is insecure, feeble, or trivial, small-spirited, powerless.

Wrong.

We are, by our love, the embodiment of dignity and power. When we run with those deep passions we are fire, water, earth; the air around us ignites with energy.

Our love filets our souls and rips our heart out of our chest walls, but that essential opening is the beginning of wisdom.

Our love is harbored in our molecules. It is deeper than emotion, more potent than action, more profound than knowing.

Our love is joyous, grand, luscious, generous, gracious, opulent, extravagant, inconsolable, ardent, willful, intense, passionate, lavish, playful, regal, miraculous, terrible in its strength, majestic in its conduct, the essence of fire.

A week before Christmas 1990, the mall is glazed with frenetic red and green lights, the forced merriment of oddly hung tinsel, a faux gaiety. The plaintive "I Saw Mommie Kissing Santa Claus" hovers in the air. I am more tired than I had imagined I could be. My feet hurt. As does my heart. My father died in the middle of November, and I am trying to deal with Christmas all in one night. It is late, only an hour before the mall closes.

Coffee and a minute off these feet are necessary. I find a shop that sells fresh hazelnut coffee, soothe the coffee with a little cream, and take it to a bench overlooking a large open area. This perch is a little sanctuary, a place to get my mind off the loss and the tasks, too many of them yet ahead. Not much joy in the scurry downstairs, I notice. The faces look as tired and feverish as mine feels. Shoppers are swept away in the flood of brown, black, and dark blue coats. The view is a short course in dismay.

Down the corridor a bit, a flash of bright red catches my eye; it is a Santa hat with white fur around the rim, a puff ball at the tail. The face under it is gracious with middle years and merry. The woman is small and a little round, and she holds a dark-haired boy, about three years old, in her lap. Obviously, grandmother and grandson are planted there to entertain each other while the rest of the family shops. She tells him a story, and then he tells her a story. They talk almost nose to nose. Their eye contact with each other is sustained and lovely. The boy is patting her face with a small fat hand, the way children do when they are at the heart of tenderness.

Oblivious to the flood of people around them, to the tinkly music, the fake Christmas trees, the whirring of credit card transactions, *they are love.* Thoughts race through my head as they do when learning is intense: Christmas is real no matter what we do to it or what happens to us. Little boys and girls need stories, long-held hugs, and the undivided attention of their matriarchs.

Love is the most potent energy on the planet.

Our Glory Years' love is growing large enough to lose its neediness; large enough to lose self-consciousness; large enough to embrace the world. We get to listen to the breath and the beat of the heart, heed the story inside the story, the one held back, the one that whispers softly the truth. It turns out to be the same breath, the same story, the same heartbeat.

Our story, our breath, our heart.

Our love, for all its tenderness, is the embodiment of strength and will. It carries us through the tasks of caring for our parents as they age, no matter how hard, how demanding, how imperative those tasks are. It supports our teens as they rampage through the dark side, trying to find their way into themselves, no matter how grueling, how heart-wrenching, how scary that is. Our love builds a community of shelter and care for the poor and the uneducated. It creates a community of artists and the practice of art.

Our moaning prayers for peace help bring war to a close.

Our love demands justice. It demands healing. It demands integrity.

No matter what.

Whatever care, regard, or trust we extend to the world comes back to us. Love is a 360-degree circle – *everything we send out* – returns.

Our perception of life shifts as we age; we see the wonder in living beings more often. We begin to sense our own vulnerability and frailty, and, further, we recognize the moments of grace, beauty, compassion, wit, generosity, and forgiveness in people everywhere. Love leaves us with a profound sensibility of just being one of Mama God's kids, in immediate danger of losing dimensions and boundaries, distances and distractions. We often dissolve into puddles of love for every apparent reason.

Glory Years' women are telling their stories now; every story is another degree or two of love that we understand. Glory Years' love is at the center of a formidable power: women's love, of all the women alive on the planet today, and all of the women who have ever lived – our collective love, from everywhere and from all time, forms the full circle of love, love with an immense and unsatisfied power. Women's love – whether it is sexual or maternal, social or political, fierce or tender – comes from a core of our concern for all of life.

Our love has the power to alter the harm that is the bequest of history.

Our love provides hope where none exists.

Our love finds a way where no way was.

Our love bears the force of gravity.

Mira is at in the mall, wandering in a small shop that sells crystal salad bowls, Royal Doulton china, and sterling silver. She looks over the gifts, hoping to find something for the family matriarch, the grande dame who still uses white linen for Sunday dinners. A boy about three years old walks a few steps away from a woman who might be his grandmother. Mira recognizes harm or neglect instantly. He has dirty hair and a terrible haircut; his hair sticks out in different lengths, some of them quite long, all over his head. If he has cut his own hair, no one has taken him to a barber to even it out, or even given him a shampoo in several days. His face is messy, and his eyes are caked with the remnants of sleep. His clothes look like they'd had a week's worth of wear.

But his eyes are so sad, an unabating sadness. Mira says that if she could have picked him up and carried him from the store, she would have. But the grandmother seems fine to her, quiet and reasonable in her approach to the boy. Still something is scary wrong.

So Mira does the best she can. She pours out her energy to the boy, drenching him in all the love she can muster, flooding him in prayer and hope and comfort and promise. She and the boy sustain eye-contact across the shop for a momentary eternity. She sends all she is, all she has.

The grandmother calls the boy to her. As the boy walks toward the grandmother, he walks also toward Mira and reaches out to touch her coat as he goes by.

This is one degree of love Mira is sure about: love is an energy people can feel even when there is a distance between them, even when no words can be spoken, even when they are utter strangers who will never see each other again.

> We are meant to keep the home fires burning, the fires in our hearts. We are meant to prepare the food, the spiritual food of love and compassion. We are meant to care for the children, not just our own, but every child. When we do not recognize our cosmic function, our own hearts break, and so does the heart of the world.
>
> —MARIANNE WILLIAMSON

We talk about falling in love, when in reality we fall *into* love, a thing that is as everywhere as water, an energy as generous as sky. If we are very, very lucky, the most subtle shift of consciousness occurs sometimes in our Glory Years. It's a degree or two of awareness that enlarges our center, our point of reference. We move from *a me and mine* sensibility to a *we and ours* sensibility. And the *we* turns out to be immense.

We are everything and always.

Pianos with the silent F-sharp and the out-of-tune middle C. Long grasses on windswept prairies. Snickerdoodles. Lost children in Bosnia. Potato latkes. Old Faithful. Peacocks in full plume. Crusty old farmers who tell the truth whether you want to hear it or not. My antediluvian Macintosh. Creamy Limoges teacups. Politicians and economists and lawyers, however they come. Saints and mystics and sages, however they come. Rice farmers kneeling in ankle-deep waters. The four Annies: Anne Lamott, Annie Dillard, Anne Tyler, Annie Proulx. The turquoise sea off the coast of Monterey. Wildfires in August, blazing through a tortured landscape. Paxter, my sweet old monster cat. Jazz that is joyous and rambunctious.

Everything and always.

Children writing their first poems. Amoebas. Neonatologists fighting to save the tiniest babies. Maya Angelo. Russian icons. Salt marshes. A King James Bible, autographed by my mother when she was six years old. Northern lights. African villages along the southeastern coast. The vibrant colors of Mexico and the people who wear them. Sea otters, chipmunks, and prairie dogs, the most gregarious animals on the planet. Post-it notes. German cars, French wines, Italian food. Homemade tamales served hot from a Dutch oven. Jellyfish drifting in a warm current.

Babies with brown eyes. Babies with blue eyes. Babies with golden eyes. Skiers and Kayakers.

Everything and always.

Radioactive frogs with too many toes. The people of Tibet. Cypress and sagebrush. The music of the Andes. Orion. Waitresses serving old jokes and hot coffee. AIDS patients in Africa and everywhere else. Slow-moving rivers. My aunt's banana bread. Australians. The intricate art of the Lakota women. Stories whispered and secrets softly kept. Seven-foot basketball players the color of mahogany. Asian traditional drummers. Business people who profit from the poor and the lost. And those who don't. The sister-in-law who saved our family. Our matriarchs and our patriarchs in the sky. Chocolate. The wind they call Mariah. Every best friend I've ever had.

Family, then family again.

And again family.

And then again family.

Everything and always.

As we make those subtle conscious and unconscious shifts, we lose our neediness and our self-consciousness. We radiate tenderness in every direction, becoming the whole circle, all 360 degrees, of love. We are entering an immense consciousness of love, one larger than we might have imagined. We begin to understand the force of loving-kindness as the Buddhists explain it and the majestic power behind Jesus' assertion that God is love. When we create, learn, share, or move in love, we enter the power, which is the force behind the flower that shatters the stone, a catalyst for the faith required to move mountains, even if we have to do it one teacup-full at a time, or as the agent for a hope so dogged, so persistent, so pragmatic Abba himself finally must give way.

Our love grows big and sturdy and ridiculously undiscriminating. So much of what we once thought momentous now seems silly and pretentious; now we cling to the only significant thing there is — loving well and not at all wisely.

And that changes everything.

That energy can be felt even when there is significant distance, even when no words are spoken. Enough so that children reach out to touch us. Enough so that our men lose the loneliness in their eyes. Enough so that potbellied pigs like Oscar, sensing the opportunity for a snuggle, can find us.

Even when hundreds of people surround us.

Even when the odds would be against it.

4.

Crossing into the Deep

TEN THIRTY Saturday night, I stumble through our local grocery, steering around the night crew as they shelve cans of spinach, six packs of toilet paper, and boxes of Cheerios. Thirtyish women with massive hair, leather vests, and tattoos with mixed messages cradle steaks and mushrooms (obviously, their biker pals are more middle-class than they'd like to admit). Late-term adolescents try to cajole their way into cigarettes and beer, with not much success. And the computer gamers, whose eyes are blinking hard against the fluorescents, push carts laden with Twinkies, red-hot Cheetos, buffalo wings, and high-octane Cokes.

I am buying the makings of a ham salad for a church potluck the next day and the Matriarchs in the Sky are having their way with me. The Matriarchs in the Sky are mothers, grandmothers, aunts, wise women, not so much alive in the flesh, but certainly alive in memory, perhaps in one of the mystery dimensions the mathematicians suggest. These women were Sherman tanks in lacy aprons, powerful in their rural counties – how well a woman cooked was a demonstration of her standing in the community. If she had leftovers, she'd have to carry her plastic-wrapped infamy home with her. I am a fair-to-middling cook, and potlucks throw me. I'd a bad run of leftovers.

The Matriarchs are issuing commandments.

Excuse me, offering advice.

A rice and ham salad. Easy enough, I'm thinking. I'm not so emotionally connected to a salad. I mean, if people don't like the salad, it won't be like I'd made a pie, a three-hour and a fifteen-dollar undertaking.

Two pounds of rice won't feed a hundred people, the Matriarchs whisper. *Not everybody will be able to have all they want. You know how men are – if they find something they like, they eat a lot of it.*

I pick up five pounds of rice.

Four red peppers aren't enough. Better get five.

I do as I am told.

One kind of onion isn't all that interesting, better get three.

I find red onions, leeks, and shallots scattered in different places on the produce aisle.

You're not going to use canned pineapple, now, are you?

It takes me twenty minutes to pick out the freshest, ripest

pineapple. I pull a leaf loose and then smell the end of the fruit. If it smells "pineapplely," it's ripe. I leave a pile of leaves.

The raisins are easy, but I can't find fresh mint. So I get dried and the Matriarchs suck all the air out of the room.

You'll have to get fresh mint at the co-op in the morning. That's all there is to it.

A big bunch of celery and half a pound of slivered almonds for crunch – nine dollars a pound organic – is the last of the produce.

That's not enough ham in those little packages, better get a whole ham. It'll be cheaper over the long haul – you can use the extra ham in soup.

I get a fifteen-pound ham.

Thirty-five dollars and an hour later, I get home. I still need to cook the rice. Now.

Do you know how long it takes to cook five pounds of brown rice? I park in front of *Saturday Night Live*, jerking awake periodically to check for the smell of burning rice, tumble into bed at two in the morning, trusting that the gooey brown mass will be cooked the whole way through. Raw brown rice is scattered all over the kitchen floor – when I jerked open the bag, I had a little rice fandango for a minute.

Up at five, I am slicing and dicing the ham, peeling and swearing at a goddamned pineapple, chopping, chopping, chopping – a bunch of celery, three kinds of onions, five red peppers. After scrambling through the cabinets, I discover — the hard way — that my bowls aren't big enough, so I put five pounds of cooked brown rice, half a fifteen-pound ham, a massacred pineapple, half a pound of slivered almonds, a box of raisins, and four pounds of vegetables in the bottom of my turkey roaster.

It takes me almost forty minutes to dash to our local co-op and back. I can't find the mint in its usual place, so I beg the produce manager to find the fresh mint still on the loading dock. I am a little nuts. "Potluck," I explain. He laughs.

The Matriarchs smile approvingly. *Anything for other people, they say. Nothing is too much trouble, too expensive, or too much work for the people you love.*

Back home, I chop mint like the Mad Hatter, whip canola oil and vinegar together, toss it all on the mountain of salad and stir like a whirling dervish, which I am at this point. I shred — along with the mint — my time schedule, my budget, and my sanity. Finally the whole glistening salad is perfect — substantial and delicious — a masterpiece of salty, sweet, sour, and soft and crunchy. But the kitchen is a disaster: peelings all over the counters, cooked rice sticking to the floor via the fresh pineapple juice, raw rice crunchy under that, stacks of plates, pots, bottles, knives, and spoons. There isn't time to spiff up.

But wait!

I don't have a serving bowl big enough for the salad.

Only my monstrous cast-iron wok will hold a decent amount. I heap the salad on the wok and corral the thing with five or six sheets of aluminum foil. More than half of the salad goes back into the refrigerator.

I fly off to church, substantially after eleven. (I think Father Joe might forgive me for tardiness, but I'm not so sure about swearing at a pineapple.) I'm exhausted and irritable, wondering why it is so much trouble and so costly to make a little something to share.

When I sit the salad on the table, it towers over every other dish on the table. The tin foil makes it look like R2-D2. I rush into the sanctuary in time for Communion and the last prayer. It occurs to me that God feeds us only bread and wine, and we all seem to be the better for it. After the potluck, my salad, heaping as it was, is almost gone, a validation of some sort. I'm not going down in shame.

Well done, the Matriarchs sigh a pleasure. *Now go clean up your kitchen.*

I do. Three hours to clean up the kitchen, an hour to shop, two hours to cook the rice, five hours to chop veggies, slice and dice half a ham, mixing, mixing, mixing and a trip to the co-op – that salad cost me thirty-five dollars and eleven hours of my life.

At work the next day, we host a conference on alcoholism and family dynamics. After the first round of coffee, glazed donuts, and chitchat, I clean up the tables and tidy the room, finding a list of forty-five characteristics of codependency.

I had committed forty-two of them in the last thirty-six hours.

My matriarchs were and are the grandest women I'll ever know. Their legacy is of inestimable worth. They cared about everybody so profoundly, so expertly. And yet . . .

Codependency Salad, anyone?

Sky Cracking

Sometimes the sky cracks open, the light filters through an opening in the clouds, and we finally see who we really are. Clearly, something inside my soul needed tending. Getting beyond the hubris and the folderol of my life through my own layers of resistances and impertinences was the task at hand. I needed to stop tap-dancing on the surface of my own life, to stop being the mistress of distraction and disassociation, to cross into a deeper way of life, to move from an insane state of being to a saner one. I needed to dump what was superfluous, to burn what was harmful or untrue, to engrave in my journals what was earnest and valuable and funny.

I spent a year crossing from the surface world to the world of the deep. Professional counseling was at the heart of it, but I also haunted lectures and conferences, prowling corridors where books were kept in straight lines, voices hushed. I attended to everything: what art, music, movement, stories did for my spirit; the way people looked when they were telling the truth and the way they looked when they were not; where on-the-books learning and off-the-books learning coincided and where they collided.

On-the-books learning was following a recipe for osso buco; off-the-books learning was making something of raw broccoli, leftover calamari, half a grapefruit, a handful of hazelnuts, and a box of Cajun rice – dinner on a night when I was too tired to drive to the market. On-the-books learning was practicing Bach for fifteen minutes, adhering strictly to the score; off-the-books learning was improvisation, my own jazz, played at three in the morning on somebody else's piano, fueled by yearning. On-the-books learning was reading about family dysfunction; off-the-books learning was telling the family about it.

These women led me into the deep: Anne Wilson Schaef taught me about codependency, which turned out to be a freight load of crappy little behaviors. Her work freed me from self-induced servitude. Julia Cameron introduced me to art as a pathway – a life. Candace Pert and Joan Borysenko suggested that our bodies are wonder and mystery, masquerading as flesh. Terry Tempest Williams wrote stories of unpremeditated truth, words stronger than life. Maya Angelou and Clarissa Pinkola Estes taught me that women were messengers of fire and blood. SARK invited me out to play.

My perceptions altered. And I began to see dichotomy

and paradox everywhere: to comprehend how two para-
graphs on chlorophyll could bore me silly, but chlorophyll
finding its way to the sun, under the guise of sweetly blue
flax flowers, was worthy of two hours of undeterred watching; to understand why an old man could say he is just fine,
thanks, when it was clear his alcoholism or his misspent
hope was going to bury him; and to realize that people –
mouthing platitudes about teamwork – could, in the next
instant, find ways to harm other people professionally and
personally.

"There's a disparity here," Jean Lundegaard, the mur-
dered wife in *Fargo*, sputtered. And I understood the gap.

There are at least two realities operating, maybe more.
The surface world is stultifying, and at some level, unfaith-
ful to the truth. The deep world is vital and dangerous,
inhabited by the extraordinary and the ordinary. But it is
the place where we can breathe, and the odd and broken
things of the world can reconcile and heal. The disparity
between the surface world and the deep world is vast, and
the trip from one world to another is as perilous as any trip
we'll ever undertake. Finding my way came at great cost,
but not bridging the gap had left me disoriented, depressed,
anxious, and, at times, useless on the face of the earth.

Crossing into the deep arose organically from the living
of my life. It's where I learned ultimately how responsible
I am to life; that I was world-weaving, creating my own
reality as I went along; that everything I do, everything I am

matters. It's where I took what I learned, and through practice and experience, made it what I know.

I wasn't the only woman making this journey into the depth of stories, both cultural and personal. This adamant search for health and truth, this fiery quest defines a generation. As Glory Years women crossed into the deep, we all began to understand the world differently.

This is what I learned: Politics are tricky and peculiar, more often about vested interest than common good. History was written by the victors; the victimized and the silent might have had another story altogether. Economics is a shared illusion based on assignments of worth that might not be valid. Healthy competition respects the competitors; but healthy collaboration achieves a success competitors envy. War resolves nothing. Most of what happens to us is preventable by staying away from junk food and junk living, taking a walk in the mornings, paying our bills on time and saving a little money, hugging our children and snuggling our mates. Our lives grow simpler as we grow more complex.

The body is the mind: the heart remembers, hands think and respond without conscious direction, bellies are the place of intuition and spirit, as well as the place of trepidation. When we are frightened, we cover our wombs with our arms.

The speed of light is the speed of ideas. Art, music, drama, literature are alchemical forces, altering our blood chemistry for the better and the way our minds perceive the world, particularly if we create words and images ourselves. Spirit is showing up as science these days, music as mathematics, art as light. Chaos theory suggests that life is chaos and destruction interspersed with great beauty and an astonishing order, which is as close to a description of my reality as I've ever read. Quantum physicists hint that my old blue chair, cradling me as I write these words, is nothing more than energy held together by a good idea.

These things give me both the shivers and a sense of rapture.

They come from a depth that I can barely fathom.

When I began to look at who I was and what I was about, I discovered a constant, ineffective whiner fueled by a dire malcontent, an enduring irresponsibility, a deviousness that Tolkein's Gollum would have relished, and just a hint of the dominatrix. It wasn't sexual, *I should be so lucky,* but it surely was the flick of the black whip. The demand for money, sex, and some sort of power over my own life led to exhaustion, malaise, confusion, instability, and an unbelievable anxiety. As I uncovered secrets, my own and my family's, darkly hidden and well kept, I could move a little, breathe a little.

And that was just the first layer.

Next came a layer of vulnerability and fragility and a

veil of fear. These middle layers were the hardest to get through, as they felt sticky and intractable. It was the place I got stuck and stayed stuck until I could feel the fear the way a blind woman feels the face of a child, a delicate exploration accomplished with tenderness. I learned that fear and vulnerability melt in the presence of kindness, especially when other people are kind to us, more especially when we get strong enough and brave enough to be kind to ourselves, most especially when we are kind to someone else.

I was of the view – who knows where I picked this up? – that our deeper layers would be fraught with worms as significant as Gollum. But that was wrong. Our deepest self is whole and holy.

Perhaps our souls are like ponds. The green slime is all on top. Underneath, we are fecund, mysterious, quiet – still. This is the place of our birthing, our creativity, integrity, our truth.

And deeper still –

Serenity.

Untangling Our Stories

"Well," Alicia leans over the sink and washes her hands. She's blond, dressed in a silk jacket of vibrant reds and oranges, and her hair is cropped short around a strong face. We're standing in a bronzed bathroom of a restaurant, after a dinner out with our book club. (The inside joke: in our fifties, we still don't go to restrooms by ourselves.) The book club has been discussing Edith Wharton's *The House of Mirth*. The story leaves me feeling listless, powerless, empathetic for women whose only option was a suitable marriage. As the women of that era aged, that option disappeared. Unmarried at fifty, they starved or relied on the kindness of strangers. Family, if they were lucky.

"I've reached that stage of life," Alicia says. "I'm bored and restless and I need to do something different with my life. So it's either have an affair or go back to school. I really like my husband, so I think I'll get a Ph.D."

I smile.

Just when we're supposed to be tired, a little out of it, millions of Glory Years women are tackling the big things: advanced degrees, learning new languages, taking up a craft or an art, or sorting out a contrary family history. Perhaps a new life calls to us. Or we're jarred by an unfamiliar experience, one that requires a new point of view and subsets of knowledge and skill. Maybe life requires a deepening compassion for the tangles of human behavior.

Whatever it is, we open up like baby birds with their beaks upraised for breakfast. We might take our sweet old husbands to Europe for a six-week stay at a language immersion school. Or we decide whether we want to tackle snowboarding or jazz piano. The facts, the nuances, the connections stay with us longer, and we get them quicker. Learning alters our neurons which alters our physiology which alters who we are at our most basic levels. We learn with pleasure.

I wanted a new craft, one with texture and color that required concentration. Coming from a legion of northern European women – Welsh, Irish, German, English – my mother, grandmothers, aunts all did *something* with their hands to occupy the evening. So I'm learning to knit, a thing that links me to the voices and the memories of my matriarchs.

I've made a startling number of twelve-foot scarves for friends and family over the last year. Twenty, maybe. An old art in new hands. My guess is this: there's an infinity of permutations as you learn to knit, more than all the grains of sands in the Sahara, layers of chaos and order that only make sense as you complete the pattern.

We're at a dinner theater in a renovated warehouse. The ceiling and the pipes are painted black, the old oak floor covered by a dove gray indoor-outdoor carpet, the ancient bricks are painted a muted wine, but the white table cloths and wine glasses gleam in the soft light. The stage dominates the end of the room; the red velvet curtain is still closed. The lights are turned up over the audience. We chat with our tablemates as the costumed actors serve us roast beef and mashed potatoes, then trek up and down the worn stage steps a thousand times, as performers do when they are nervous and aren't quite sure what to do with their bodies, where to put their hands, whether to dance or hop, whether to evaporate on the spot or simply spontaneously combust.

An actress I know slightly, comes to our table. She's dressed in a floor-length black velvet gown, poofed with crinolines, littered with rhinestones. The fabric swishes when she walks. She wears an extravagant hat, a thick choker of jewels clustered at her throat and wrist in the manner of seventeenth-century Swedish aristocracy.

"I've had *that* birthday, you know," the actress says. "I needed to ignite an old passion, singing in musical theater or light opera. Although why I need this little mayhem, I don't know just yet. It scares me, and on another level, it suits me. I'm very nervous. This is opening night and my first performance since college."

We're seeing a production of *A Little Night Music* by Steven Sondheim, whose music is wickedly difficult, both in melody and lyric. This is a beloved story, the finding of true love sometime in your fifties, with all the requisite quirks, misadventures, and backtracks. "Send in the Clowns" comes from this musical. Our actress floats serenely as a cloud on stage, her black gown as fluid as her performance, her voice perfect for the aching wisdom in Sondheim's music. Note by tentative, graceful, soaring note.

At first, I worry my hands around the needles and the yarn, ordering their every move. I fuss at the craft as if the needles are foreign and my fingers don't understand the language. Early learning feels like hell. I tell my brain to tell my hands to wrap the loop around the needle. And that is knitting. I don't purl until my fifth or sixth scarf, and it feels bass-ackwards for a long time. I am determined not to quit, but moving forward doesn't seem like a good idea either.

Intention. Action. Completion.

A new integrity for me.

There's been a fuss over an aborted performance a year ago; a friend's brilliant work was treated with disrespect. We had been trying to find space and time for this performance at our local book fest. Josephine was the new coordinator. Mary, a singer-songwriter and poet, had written a magnificent hour-long reader's theater, a profoundly moving piece on women's history. In the end, we were offered a ten-minute time slot at ten o'clock on a Saturday night.

Every one had taken the rejection in stride, except me. I boiled over and it wound up in an e-mail that was sent to Josephine. I was profoundly embarrassed, and Josephine, who was at the other end of the tangle, carried the wound for over a year.

We are trying to sort this out over coffee. She apologizes for creating the disrespect – without excuse, explanation, or rancor, takes responsibility with grace, humility, and honesty.

I am amazed by this turn. I'd expected, well, another thing.

"All we really needed was a good solid no," I say. "Telling us upfront that our presentation would not work for you would have been really helpful. We wouldn't have fussed."

"I didn't know how to do that then. I'm learning," Josephine admits.

"I understand, I've been there. We accept and appreciate your apology."

The hour we thought we needed to untangle this mess turned in less than five minutes into a chat between friends over the issues of our lives as writers. I tell her about this book, this essay. She tells me of her poetry, her children, her life in two states: a marriage in one, work in another.

"I'm working differently than I've ever worked before," she says, "staying true to my own life. I think midlife women are growing fast and hard in the ways of integrity, meaning, connection. We're learning at the speed of light. We're such late bloomers, such strange blossoms."

I've made a tangle of things. A tiny slipped stitch nine inches back left a huge hole which requires an unraveling. Four rows make an inch, each row requires a yard of yarn – I unravel thirty-six yards. As I begin to knit the scarf back together again, I naively think that order will find its way out of chaos. I am so wrong. It tangles majestically in less time than it takes for me to type this sentence. Less time than it takes for the human heart to skip a beat.

"When Dad moved out of his house into the nursing home, we found evidence of a marriage we didn't know about," Margaret explains. "And another brother. Apparently, Dad had gotten his girlfriend pregnant at the end of high school. They married before the baby was born, and divorced soon after. He abandoned that child. I asked my mom if she knew about this other child, this other marriage. She knew – and never told."

Margaret and her seven brothers and sisters, flustered by the news of a previous marriage and another sibling, email furiously, and decided that they would find their other brother. Margaret's younger brother, Jim, took this on as a quest and found Mike, who turned out to be a jewel of a guy eager to connect with his eight new brothers and sisters. He accepted financial and emotional responsibility for his newly recovered dad. Some men have an endless capacity for forgiveness and for offering a great good in place of harm. This one did, at any rate.

Sorting out the tangle, I tumble into the strange craft of string-following. I start at the nib of the string and follow it as far as it takes me. Sometimes the yarn seems to fly out of my hands, at others, I am profoundly, irrevocably stuck. It takes courage to plunge into the heart of a knot with a hundred tentacles, pulling at one and then another, until something loosens. Instead of getting easier, the knots get more obtuse and I get crankier. But I've found that I go a long way – a little bit at a time.

"And then we found evidence of another child, an out-of-wedlock child this time. This child was fathered when Dad was about sixteen. And another truth emerged from my mother – the reason my parents divorced was because of infidelity. Lifelong infidelity it turns out; perhaps there were other children born outside of my parents' marriage. That's not clear now.

"My family wanted to find this new child and I shouted, 'Stop! I don't want to know how many more brothers and sisters we have. It's too much. It's better to just let this lie. Some of these people have to be in their sixties. If somebody asked me how many brothers and sisters I have, I'd have to say 'I don't know.'"

I asked Margaret where she was in the birth order now. "I used to be fourth, now I'm down to seventh or eighth. There are ten of us that we know about. We don't know if he fathered more children while he was married to my mom, and there were eight of us. He spent three years in Guam during World War II, so we could have a multiracial family, when we thought we were all Irish Catholics. And then there was the time between his divorce and remarriage. There could easily be fifteen or twenty of us scattered all over the world. You never know what you don't know.

"And get this. Last week at the nursing home, my eighty-two-year-old father captured an Alzheimer's patient so he could have sex with her. She was willing, apparently. He has Parkinson's disease so it took him a long time to shuffle in his walker to the door and lock it, and come back to the bed. It's only a few steps. Then he was undressing his 'girlfriend.' That's when he was caught."

Margaret pauses for a moment, "I have a father who is a one-trick pony."

I eventually untangle all thirty-six yards of yarn. There are plenty of missed opportunities, misspent hopes, the usual number of backtracks and blind alleys, days of being simply stuck. String-following takes me where I need to go at a pace I can stand. Eventually, everything resolves one way or another. I confess that on a few occasions I left an indisputable knot, hidden deep in the patterns, an imperfection that saves the whole.

I wander into an antique store: there are early twentieth-century salt-and-pepper shakers that look like the *Katzan-jemmer Kids*, crocheted doilies, pink Fiestaware, green mason jars, a coffeepot blackened from use over an open campfire. A woman sits at the front desk, fiddling with papers, bringing them close to her face, holding them away. I stop to say hello and notice that her eyes don't work in the expected way and that her speech inflections are different as well. I worry that she might be having a stroke. Never one to ignore the elephant on the couch, I ask the woman if she is all right.

"I'm more than fine," she laughs. "I've only been able to see and hear for a few weeks."

"How – ?"

"I was born deaf, and I lost my sight to cataracts a few years back. I had cataract surgery three months ago, a cochlear implant about a month ago."

"Do sounds drive you crazy? Does what you see unnerve you?"

"I have hearing aids and I can turn them down if I need to, especially here at the shop. The sounds of big trucks rumbling by terrify me. And I turn it up when I'm in my backyard. I never knew how noisy crows could be. Seeing again, well, I had the memory of sight so it's like revisiting an old world. This afternoon I'm headed to my backyard, listening for robins and sparrows, crows and magpies, doves and bobwhites, and those noisy little squirrels. I'm learning the world all over again."

It's quiet, early in the day. I don't yet have my glasses on, so I pull the needles close to my eyes. I hear a tiny explosion of bamboo against bamboo where the needles connect. A swish takes the yarn from one needle to the other.

I can trace the wool back to the little shop nestled under old trees, set back from a busy highway, trace it back to the loom and the alpaca; back to the winter ranges and the summers pastures in the Andean mountains; back to air and sun, blue grass and green water. Making fabric from two sticks and a string is a primitive art.

I love the softness of the wool, in colors like wine or sunset or pewter, colors that strut from the imagination. The patterns make sense, and the shape of the stitches tells me where I am and what I need to do next. I can work my way through the worst of tangles and, in the process, create order and beauty and warmth. "Knitting a sweater is a tremendous act of faith," writes Bernadette Murphy in her book, *Zen and the Art of Knitting*. It's a quiet, slow way of learning the world.

A black-and-white wool forms patterns resembling the night sky, a scattering of stars here and there, softened by patches of clouds. Nothing very much happens when I knit, nothing very hard or very fast. My mind, usually tangled by time and space and obligation, untangles, settles, focuses, and slips into its rightful place. The yarn, not much more than a whisper thick, loops effortlessly around the needles and endows emptiness with a habitation and a function.

Learning as We Go

Under the canopy of a city park, next to the rose garden, a group of children huddle around picnic tables to write. We are at a summer writing camp, helping nine through eleven year olds come to value their own stories. Dawn, a New Yorker with a doctorate in French history, is teaching with an abundance of high energy and good will. Her lessons are vital and the kids love her. The assignment is to make up imaginary words and meanings. Their words are fabulous: *buckly*, a person who only has bad luck; *coocor*, a person who is not cuckoo.

The students are doing assignments in groups of twos and threes, but they are having trouble concentrating. Three rambunctious boys, Mason, Jeremy, and Jack, are doing their talented best to raise hell. Jack particularly is disruptive, his whiny voice screechy in both octaves and decibels.

So the kids spread out, sitting under the trees, trying to give Jack a wide berth.

"Jack *is* cuckoo," Mackenzie, my niece, says later. She's about had it with his shenanigans.

"No, I don't think he's cuckoo, but he has a monstrous amount of energy and he misdirects it. But he's receptive as a peeled grape. He might be a buckly."

Jack is going into the fourth grade, small and dark-haired, the child with the unquiet heart. Wearing dark-rimmed glasses, he's a spitting image of Harry Potter, his hero of the moment.

"Do you ever wish you were magic?" I ask Jack. He responds by popping Mason with the backside of a notebook. "Yeah, I want to make him disappear." I have to separate them.

Jack adopts the two older boys, although neither wants him as a friend. Over the course of the week, though, his high jinks, good humor, and high drama win them over. In spite of his inability to sit still, or shut up for that matter, and his absolute mastery at turning a small disciplinary problem into a major incendiary event, he can do his assignments in record time. They are wonderfully done, his penmanship is neat and clear – miraculous for such a chaotic child.

On the last day of camp, I let up on the discipline and let the kids wander a bit and play together. They are visiting with Dawn, who is reviewing their poetry. Jack has finished with his assignments and wants to go find oak trees. We point out the shapes of leaves of an oak, but he is on the lookout for acorns and their little brown caps. "Acorns come down in the fall and this grass has been mowed a hundred times," I caution. But Jack is in one of his quieter spells and wants to go find them. "You have to stay where I can see you." He agrees.

He comes back with four or five little brown acorn caps and uses them as whistles, which instantly irritates every other child at the table. I am ready to scold him *again* for noise, when words came out of my mouth I don't expect.

"I learned something new today, Jack. Show me how to blow the whistle." He is patience itself, teaching me how to hold my thumbs, how to bend them so the air would whistle through a little space between them. I have to practice, but I finally get it. The other kids pick up the caps and learn how to do it too. Jack is transformed into the wise, gentle teacher.

Later I need to get ice cream for the kids, so I ask Jack if he wants to come with Mackenzie and me. At our grocery store Jack says, "I want to buy you and Mackenzie something, maybe for two dollars."

"A candy bar would be perfect. Please buy something for yourself too."

Jack buys candy bars for Mackenzie and me, and for the two boys that have befriended him. On the way back to writing camp, Mackenzie and I are eating candy bars at eleven o'clock in the morning, a thing we'd never done before.

"Can you believe this?" I ask her. She giggles. "Thanks, Jack!!!" we shout – replicating his usual mode of communication. Jack grins, his chocolate smile touching the rim of his glasses.

When we get back to camp, he wants to share something with his teacher as well, so he gives her half of his own candy bar. The rest of the morning we practice for the reading that night. After that, it is the time to say good-bye to the kids and to tell our students what spectacular people they are, what good work they can do. Jack is missing.

Later in our literary center Jack dashes through the reception room where I am sitting. "Jack!" I shout and hold open my arms. The boy who made me so angry folds himself into my arms and holds on for a long time. "Jack, you are a wonderful writer." He accepts the compliment with the solemnity of a rabbi.

My guess that the yelling, correcting, and cajoling, the frustration, anger, and nagging were also part of our lesson. Jack made me earn the right to tell him the good news. The deep nudged me into an unpremeditated kindness, and then the universe broke open, and anything, everything became possible.

I kiss the top of his head, and he is gone.

What We Know for Sure

Our beloved Oprah asked us what we knew *for sure*. The question is a good one. I asked other Glory Years women what they knew for sure, what the deep has taught us all. This is their list:

Our passions ignite our lives.

Compassion is the pathway to the truth.

Exercise and decent food are the ground forces of life.

We love our children no matter what.

This body is the only one I'll have.

We are capable of anarchy and mayhem, and both have their uses.

If our minds and hearts are closed, neither love nor money can get to us.

Our children deserve our best selves.

Money helps.

Good-hearted men abound on this planet.

We can't do it alone. Whatever "it" is.

Anything can happen at any time.

The consequences call the shots.

A good cry is a good thing.

Money helps.

Hard laughter is as necessary as bread.

Cheap clothes are expensive.

What is loved loves back.

What is hated hates back.

Integrity is power.

Organization is power.

Creativity is power.

True love is a force to be reckoned with.

A single kiss can alter the course of a life.

Popeye was right about spinach.

Money helps.

Calamities and tragedies teach us what is essential about
    life—and what isn't.

The only sanity is love; the only stability is truth.

This is what I know for sure.

Everything in our lives has meaning: all of our miswhacks and our leaps of faith; all of our laughter, tears and
prayers; every action taken by our hands; every thought
originating from our minds; every spoken word and all of
the unspoken ones.

WOMAN NOT ON PROZAC
For a long time, I wanted to be Somebody.
a person, a place, a thing,
with a Capital letter.
Hungry for direction, definition, destination.
I searched the depths and the heights,
for the why of the why seven times deep.

Because I was
out of kilter with the people around me.
An artist in a colony of pragmatists,
a liberal in a conservative community,
a woman in a family of men,
a thunderstorm in a clinic.

Because I was
fond of substance and vitality,
things shadowed, things in held in light.
good at stories, space, silence, solitude,
graceful when it didn't matter,
awkward when it did,
charmed by the decidedly odd,
left-handed turns and travels south,
enamored by the profound and the profane,
often not knowing which was which,
hooked on genuine enthusiasms which
alienated the bored, the abstracted,
the plodders, and the fearful
seven directions at once.

The price of the search was well paid
by the outer layer of my skin,
chunks of my cerebrum
and the left ventricle of my heart.
What I got was a path, a brace of soul,
a heartbeat, a sharp intake of breath,
a place to plant my feet and a few flowers,
a home in my own mind.

Who was the Somebody I wanted to be?
Astonishingly,
the answer doesn't mean much any more,
anchored as I am
in the few things that matter:
Communion. Creation. Covenant.
Compassion. Courage.

What I am today I won't be tomorrow.
Whatever nuance, presence I harbor today
will be washed away by the
tides of a new revelation
or old perception resurfacing,
random experience,
a kiss from a good man,
the opening of a rose, the scent of sage,
stone truth told by children.

What I have, feel, and do will change,
depending on the weather outside,
and the storms within.
What I am on any given day is enough.

All I have is time and all I do is
initiation, maintenance, closure,
as liquid an endeavor as there ever was.

Hearts can go sour,
dreams can turn bad,
minds can play the fool,
but problems resolve and so do people.
Wishes, more often than not, come true.
Bodies and minds heal.

We learn as we go and we are not
any the worse for doing it that way.
At rock bottom,
there is always Love
and there is always Tomorrow.

So it's enough to be fluid,
to live fully moment by moment,
to be present and accounted for,
to think clearly and act quickly,
to trust what is.

Because life is a path
and we are only graceful
when we move.

Charting Progress

On an August evening, after ten at least, the Logghe Gals are sitting on a second-story deck hugging the front of a house surrounded by sagebrush and cheat grass. It feels like we are eating dinner in a tree house – the branches of an ancient blue spruce lace over the deck. It's dark, and the lights go out periodically, which we turn back on by wildly waving our hands. The motion detector comes on with, well, you know.

We've come together to plan a workshop for Joan Logghe, a poet, and an artist-in-residence in New Mexico. Joan has been our writing teacher for five years or so, and she's made it safe for us to tell the truth of our lives in print. Our work with her is an internal gyroscope which always brings us back to center, a compass which always points true north.

Two of us are therapists. Most of us have master's degrees, two have doctorates. One is a nurse, three are full-time writers, four sing beautifully, the rest of us do not. Three of us are ardent community activists. We are conservative and liberal, Democrat and Republican. We've all been teachers of one sort or another, at some point in our lives. Learning runs in our blood.

We are Buddhist, Mormon, Catholic, Protestant, Jewish; one of us believes in quantum physics; our youngest talks to gnomes and fairies – we're not entirely sure she's kidding. Two of us are recent escapees from dangerous marriages, one of us is newly widowed, three have enduring marriages, one is newly married, one of us has four children, three of us have two, three are grandmothers, two of us are doting aunts. One of us is thirty – the rest of us are not.

We are poets, essayists, novelists, journalists, singer-songwriters, and storytellers.

We share our stories as well as succulent food: a corn-bread and veggie casserole, greens from the garden, a Chardonnay, an iced tea spiked with cinnamon.

None of us has had an easy life. Stories surface of incest, poverty, betrayal, death, madness, of an astonishing lack of love, of being lost on the face of the earth, then the finding of our way. These are stunning stories for women who are so solid, kind, responsible, and brave. Our stories have saved us – along with a deep commitment to family and community, to work, to education and creation, and to a sustaining spirituality, however we found it.

Our stories help us close the gap between the surface world and the world of the deep. Learning to tell our stories and then taking them seriously has helped us stop trivializing our lives and the lives of other people. We bring our weathered and illuminated selves to the fullness of responsibility. We've become dignity, worth, transcendent progress, authentic power. Carolyn See wrote this: "Every word a woman writes changes the story of the world, revises the official version."

Earlier in the evening, I read the Codependency Salad story. The women laugh and start to tell their "Matriarchs in the Sky" stories. Their stories are both rueful and intensely funny, reflecting both the love we have for our mothers and the places where we had to machete our way through the family undergrowth.

Now we're nibbling on dessert – my contribution: vanilla ice cream and homemade sugar cookies. Fresh blackberries, the gift of the therapist who lives by the river, make ordinary sugar cookies and vanilla ice cream a succulence.

"You know," I tell them, "I made these cookies in forty-five minutes. I whipped up the cookie dough this morning, froze it all day, and then baked the cookies in about half an hour this afternoon. I bought the ice cream. The whole thing cost me about eight dollars and took less than an hour."

They clap and cheer for me – hoots and whistles. Their applause means as much to me as anything I've ever received. These women know I am charting progress, that I am honoring the ritual of potluck, my Matriarchs, *and* being true to my own needs to not spend much time or too much money.

Nothing is too much trouble, too expensive, or too much work for people you love, the Matriarchs said, and they believed it. What feels better to me is this: *the people I love need my attention, not a bucket of ham salad.* Sometimes things are too much trouble, too expensive, or too much work. What I've learned by crossing into the deep has become a knowing that alters my behavior, the cells in my body, my life.

Our Matriarchs are hovering in the night sky. They whisper, "We wish we had known your freedom." As they pass in front of the stars, they reveal where they are by what their shadows conceal.

The shift occurs when we cross into the deep. An edge leaves us – the need to pop the whip, the need to be in control, the need to be right leaves us. We become partners and pilgrims. The insistent and enduring need to seek out what's under the surface makes us acolytes to life. No matter how old we get, life is still new to us, as if we are seeing with new eyes and hearing with new ears.

Crossing into the deep ripens us into wisdom, living now in the oxygenated cells of our blood, the marrow of our bones, the white-heat center of our core. What we've learned makes us a walking poetry, not the prissy and some-times ethereal poetry that passes for art. We are the poetry of fire and blood, the glory of light. The fiery search burned away the inessential and revealed the God-awful and the God-given truths of our lives – which, with inexplicable grace, Glory Years women weave into blessing.

There are no words for such courage.

5.

This One Thing

THE AIR IN MY lungs is clear, clean, cold. Fall air. Mountain air. I am at our local ski resort, Bogus Basin, forty-five-straight-up minutes from Boise. The long dry grasses are mottled with gold and softened with cream, the pines pungent and invigorating.

We are close to sky here. Light on the mountain is different, more beguiling, than light on flat land. It is translucent, luminous – fragile like ancient Chinese porcelains.

The pines fret softly as the wind blows in from the north. Even though it's October, the tamarack and the aspen have yet to change, though their greens are faded with the altitude and the season. A Steller's jay settles on a nearby post.

I relish this day in the mountains. I'm about to teach a

journaling class to cancer patients, survivors, and their care-givers – nurses, therapists, and physicians. I worry about intruding into wounded psyches; the women are a blending of fragility and strength, the by-product of cancer survival.

The morning before I'd been to my sculpting class. "What could I possibly tell cancer survivors about heal-ing?" I asked my teacher, Surel, who battles the dual demons of lupus and multiple sclerosis. She told me that "when you are ill, your identity changes, and the role of the journal is to rediscover who you are." I reeled with the insight, dashed home, and rewrote my whole presentation in two hours.

Identity issues I know about.

This morning, leaning against the mountains I trust, I pray that each woman will take what she needs and disre-gard the rest.

Journaling is like prayer or exercise; it seems innocuous enough at first take. Once or twice won't hurt you, but if you become serious about it, everything in your life will change. Six days of journaling won't do it, but six months out you begin to notice that you are different, and people respond to you differently. In six years, nothing in your life will be the same. You'll explode miserable relationships and nightmarish jobs, and pick your way through the debris, word by tenuous word, until you find a better place to plant your feet, like mountaintops and long straight roads to the horizon.

After lunch, forty or so women settle into the dining area in the lodge. The room is lined by windows, and the mountain outside them is close enough to reach out and touch. An eternity of soft browns and grays, the valley where we all live stretches out before us. At the horizon are the violet Owyhee Mountains, which can disappear and reappear right before our very eyes, given the light of the day and the clouds and fog that can erase their presence. The fall haze is a magician.

I sit on the floor. The women gather around me. Most of them sit cross-legged, a few in chairs. I warn them that we will be traveling on dangerous ground, that we need to acknowledge the harrowing times which also birth our stronger, kinder selves. I read a passage from *A Walk Between Heaven and Earth*. The author was writing about the death of her brother and her visceral grief.

> In my own journals I saw that, after years of writing, things began to change . . . . At any rate I noticed that the charts and maps I now make of my inner wilderness are different. Some benevolence has entered, a deep affection of those unknown territories, some strange conversion of danger into poetry.
>
> —BURGHILD NINA HOLZER

After the women write a bit, they read some of their work.
I ask them to write down these words:

> *The part of me that is angry,*
> *the part of me that is sad,*
> *the part of me that is afraid,*
> *is the part of me that is a*
> *powerful force working*
> *to ensure my survival.*

Maddie, a woman in her twenties, her softness and youth
at odds with her black leather motorcycle jacket and male
affectation says this, "I don't believe those words."

"Write them in the back of your journal, Maddie," I say.
"Look at them every once in awhile, just let them feed you."

She writes the words down and then she starts to cry.
"My cancer is back. I went through four years of chemo,
and I don't think I have the courage or the strength to do it
again." She is sitting on the floor, hunched over in a fetal
position, the way very young children curl up when they
are demoralized.

"Maddie, anyone who has survived four years of chemo
is the epitome of strength and courage," I say. The faces
of the women in the circle are intent, an embodied compassion. "How many of you agree with that?" I ask. Every
woman in the circle raises her hand. "Maddie, look up. Look

at the validation of your strength." Maddie looks up at the
raised hands, sniffs back her tears. She smiles a wobbly
smile.

The second session only four women join me, three of
whom are the sickest, most fragile women in the whole
group. We sit outside. A dark-haired young woman cannot
manage a stable body temperature, even though it is a warm
afternoon. Her friend helps her with a blanket. The other
two women are so frail they look and move as if their bones
will crumble.

I begin the exercises, gingerly, I know I am treading on
hallowed ground, ground that could also give way and swal-
low any one of us.

The women are resistant. One of the exercises is a list-
ing of the things that we love – the things that sustain us,
bind us to this gentle old Earth. The young woman cannot
tell me one thing, not a single thing that she loves: not children, not the mountains and the golden aspen, velvet roses,
almond macaroons or fresh peach cobbler, not her parents,
her husband, her friend that supports her through her
cancer. Instead she spits out a platitude, "Our god is a jealous god."

I'm wondering if she wants to die, if she's endured so
much pain and illness that she's reached the plateau where
she has had enough, but I have sense enough not to say it.
Then I ask a question that allows for the telling of their

histories: "What experience in your life most explains why you're here?" Then the agony pours out — stories of toxic parents, terrible accidents, children in trouble, busted marriages, gods that have forsaken them, terror piled on tragedy piled on despair.

Their bodies are the mirror image of their lives.

But their stories do not have the ring of the confessional, nor are they grappling with the Fates. Maddie was the grappler. These stories have the ring of litany — a list repeated over and over again for the benefit of their doctors, their nurses, their social workers, their family and friends, their priests, and, now, me.

I feel as if I have been hit.

That evening I email a friend, a surgeon who's been watching people heal and disintegrate for twenty years, listening to their litanies, demanding that his patients get up and walk: emotionally, intellectually, physically, spiritually. I ask this: "What is the difference between a person who can realize the harm, but then let go and move on — and one who cannot?"

His response the next day: "Death, spiritually and in reality."

I mourn for the woman who could not find a single thing to love, except her jealous god. I ache for the harm these women endured in their lifetimes. I grieve that such a terrible disease should inflict its deadly terror in their already decimated lives.

But I am deeply chagrined.

I have a litany of my own.

The Litany

My troubles started before I was born, as is the way of generational things. My paternal grandparents were homesteaders, adventurers, renegades, and idealists. Their families had settled in northern Idaho just before the turn of the century. My grandmother, of German descent, was part of a Christian idealistic community – the Church of the Brethren, spiritual cousins of the Mennonites and the Amish. My grandfather was of English descent; his mother's picture indicates a dour woman with stern opinions. For such plainspoken, God-fearing people, my grandparents had a surprisingly lusty union. The evidence: postcards they had sent each other before their marriage, something they'd consummated sometime before their vows. They birthed five children, two boys and three girls.

But harm resided within that marriage.

My grandmother's family name was Hess. Rudolph Hess, one of Hitler's primary henchmen, was, in all probability, a not-too-distant cousin. It was part of our family's whispered mythology. Years into my adulthood, I saw a special on public television about his life; his blue eyes, facial structure, and dark hair strongly suggested blood ties. His contrary nature – violence and arrogance on one side, an inexplicable, perhaps fatalistic, turn away from the Nazis on the other – was a familiar theme in my German family.

We are good at inexplicable turns.

The Brethren were pacifists, and the German role in the two world wars was a torment and a shame to Grandma Herrick. Although she was a second-generation German-American citizen, she suffered the taunts of prejudice from her northern Idaho neighbors – enough that her family eventually moved to California, and then back to southern Idaho. She repeatedly found "reasons" to hit the children who carried the dark-haired, blue-eyed German gene: my father, my aunt, and a grandson. She was trying to beat *the hell* out of them. Then two of her children, well into adulthood, began to weaken physically – the early degeneration of muscular dystrophy, which requires that both parents have that genetic disposition. Neither grandparent had active muscular dystrophy. Grandma Herrick harbored the notion that her genes were the ones at particular fault. Otherwise healthy females can be carriers for the disease, passing the it on to their children, as well as encoding the gene in future generations. The disease is activated when both parents harbor this nasty little bombshell. Such is the luck of the draw.

When my father got sick, he was destined for both a lifetime of illness and the ramifications of physical violence. As a young man, he drove a delivery truck for a local meat packing company, riding solo through the sagebrush deserts, then unloading halves of beef on his back. Although he'd quit school when he was a sophomore in high school, he could do complex geometric equations using nothing but a stubby old pencil and a smooth piece of wood. He was a crack shot, and for years provided pheasant, duck, and deer meat for the war widows in his community – the reason those women survived the winters. I imagine that they were a little bit in love with him. (My uncle joined the war effort in Europe and Africa; my father was working in a war-critical industry – meat packing – and was spared the necessity of war.)

When my dad married my mother, in his early thirties, he was strikingly handsome: black wavy hair, dark blue eyes. He was a beautiful man, fiery in spirit, massively strong and fit. His clothes lay against his body with such elegance.

By his mid-thirties, the disease began as a weakening of his legs, later his arms. Muscular dystrophy is the wasting away of muscle cells. A dystrophy patient can tell a leg or a hand to lift or move, but the response gets slower and weaker, month by month, year by year. The muscles progressively turn to fat. There is a cough, a shuffling gate, a softening body.

My mother had the capacity to be very beautiful or very ordinary, depending upon the tenor of the day or the quality of the light around her. She was sensuous, affectionate, willful. Dad was tough to get along with, even early on. Our aunts and uncles commented often that Mama was the only person in three generations who could manage him. They were right.

My mother was the cusp of the family, sustained the men on rolled roasts, cherry pies, and the wide place in her soul where there was room for their stories, true and otherwise. She danced barefoot to Strauss waltzes, searched early spring for jack-in-the-pulpits on her parents' homestead, sent her daughter to the philharmonic in school shoes because it was better to go *now* with flat shoes than to wait for high heels, and managed the family with a raised eyebrow, snicker-doodles, hugs decades deep, and laughter that regretted nothing.

My mother's family was (and still is) a family of easy warmth. Mom was raised in the mesa apple orchards northwest of Boise. She had three brothers and sisters who loved nothing more than to have picnics under old trees, drink coffee or a cold beer, and tell stories. Laughter was the way they loved each other, their language and their music. Children would climb on the lap of any adult and stay. This gentle, unassuming love was so soft and so universal I still feel it, a palpable spirit of goodness and vitality.

We became a farm family, raised cattle, corn, hay, wheat, and carrots that blossomed in June. The bloom of a carrot is white, thick, heavy, and flat. When a field of carrots is in bloom, it looks like the most luscious white carpet. I wondered if a child could walk across it. I never tried; the long stems under the blossoms were flimsy, apparent even to a three year old.

In early summer, the green wheat was waist high to an adult. I would sneak away, crouch down on the edge of the field, just far enough in that I could see little else but grain and blue sky. I watched the wind play against the long stalks, bending and straightening them on a whim. The world was all green movement, all green grace, a dance of sweet peace.

Our home was a brick ranch house with floor-to-ceiling windows in the living room. The best place to take a nap on a winter day was in front of those windows. For a long time, we lived on our beautiful farm, surrounded by a thousand shades of green, bordered by country roads that went exactly where they were intended.

But I had an apprehension of trouble. When I was six, I dreamed I was in a room the color of lilacs, small enough for only a single bed and a chest of drawers. A curtain was stretched across the closet. Wrong, wrong, wrong, the colors were wrong for such an earthbound family as ours. And something else was wrong too. My mother was gone. Dead.

I woke up sobbing, and my mother rushed in to comfort me. But before my eighteenth birthday, the nightmare had come true. The family, or what was left of us, had moved into an apartment in the back of an old hardware store. The walls of my bedroom were the same sticky lilac, and a cotton curtain hung limply across my closet. And my mother was dead from a cerebral aneurysm. We sold the farm.

Her death was fast. We'd gone to a family picnic the Sunday before, eating fried chicken, wilted lettuce salad, and chocolate cake. The next morning she woke up with a terrible headache, slept all day, and didn't come to consciousness the next morning. The sirens — I can still remember those godawful sirens — the sirens coming from a distance. She was taken to the hospital, remained in the coma for ten days, and then died during a two-hour period when we'd slipped away to the farm.

When we arrived back at the hospital and walked down the long hall to her room, the nurses would not look at us. When my aunts and uncles told us that she'd died, my knees buckled, and I had to be carried to the waiting room couch. I remember thinking I couldn't trust my knees ever again. I don't remember what happened to my father and my brother or how they took the news. The world shrank to the space in front of my own eyes, and that was fuzzy and insubstantial.

Everything that happens after a death is exaggerated, exacerbated. Nothing is untouched. As my brother, Steve, said years later, "We all went crazy in different directions." My father's gruff exteriors solidified, and he became immobile, terrified of facing the rest of his life without my mother; in part because his disease was a horror, in part because he loved her so much.

After she died, my beloved brother drove way too fast, perhaps in too many areas of his life, and did not care if he lived or died. He lost his way at ninety miles an hour, until he met Maggie, who became his wife and gave him back his life, his sense of family, his sanity, and his strength.

In the year following my mother's death, I underwent a medical review with researchers and physicians who worked with muscular dystrophy patients and their families. They told me I was the carrier, the only one in my extended family.

If I married a man with the dystrophy gene, then my children would inherit the disease. I would pass the gene to my children, whether they had the disease or not, then to their children. I decided to end the despair and the terror that this disease had brought to my family. I would not have children. In a single year, I lost my mother to death, my father to despair, and my children to disease.

I became a walking sorrow.

Years of craziness followed. Big parts of my personality and my psyche went numb or quit functioning. Dissociation, I learned later, is what they call it. I was distracted, undirected, and chaotic, endured appalling relationships with men, suffered through terrible jobs that yielded no money and no respect, was as wild as a wayward colt and yet as constrained as a thunderstorm in a closet. That dissonance was reason enough for stagnation.

Taking care of my father was my primary mission in life

as the oldest daughter, a task set before me by my extended family, pointedly so. And I didn't think to question it. My brother helped as well, but boys get a pass on some of those obligations, after all, he had to build a career and raise a family.

I hated it, but probably not as much as Pop. We were locked in a combat that neither love or dysfunction could release us from. We were the same bullheaded, fiery souls, and we eviscerated each other. He carried a wild antagonism toward women, the result of his mother's beatings and my mother's death, and I was the recipient of that animosity, full bore at times, at others, in subtler ways that were harder to fight.

I was the dark-haired, blue-eyed child.

We are all the victims of our own worst moments.

I lived through the heady '60s and early '70s and have the battle scares, uh, scars to prove it. Most of us drank too much; I did. Most of us tried drugs. I did once, although their charm was lost on me after the first time, and I never tried them again. Most of us questioned the structures of our families, our communities, our government, and I did, too — Vietnam, the abortion wars, the equal rights amendment, Kennedy, Kennedy, King. And then Nixon. I learned to distrust — to some extent — *everything*. I watched the world disintegrate in places, then patch itself together with some meager, helpless hope. There were no paths to safety.

I wish I could tell you that I was the victim, sweet and

compliant, just trying to do my best. But that is not so. I was a full participant in the fracas: demeaning and manipulative; sneaky and self-absorbed, irresponsible and erratic, obsessed with what I did not have. Sometimes I did things that were truly wrong, stunningly stupid.

When you go through these things and then exercise the most brittle self-pity, depression and anxiety are reliable and predictable as warm milk curdling. I remember driving back from my father's house on back country roads late at night, crying and screaming, hanging onto the wheel with terrified hands. Everything within me wanted to drive into the nearest tree. That was the first depression. The second was the result of a broken love relationship in which my man had an affair with another woman. She wrote me a letter to tell me about it.

The loss of what *feels* like everything is difficult. To lose it again and again feels like madness. I was afraid I was going to go crazy. The fear had been in the back of my mind for ten years, and I was so weary with battling it that I finally decided to give into it. I lay down on my bed, mid-afternoon, and said to myself. "Okay, you can go crazy if you want to."

I waited.

Nothing.

I waited some more.

Still nothing.

Two hours. It wasn't going to happen. I wasn't going to

run buck naked down the streets yelling "Fie on you, you blood-sucking fools."

I got up and made a cup of tea.

Years later, Juanita, a professor of social work, told me that "real craziness is the luxury of chemistry." Apparently I had the right body chemistry for anxiety and depression, but was not going to suffer with unlikely words and visions.

It was time to see my way clear.

This Wasn't Easy Either

Although I probably could have used them, I chose not to get well on drugs. Instead I chose to dig up my truths and right my wrongs. First thing I asked my therapist, was this: "Am I crazy?" She laughed and said that if I had enough sense to ask the question, the answer was probably no. After we chatted a bit, she reaffirmed that I was troubled and in trouble, but I was also in my right mind, whatever that might be.

I began to understand the ramifications and the parameters of what had happened. I felt rage for the first time, and there was no containing it. I'd get in the car and yell — for miles. My rages would boil over at work and it would terrify people. I was hell on wheels with my family. In some instances, I was the perfect little pleaser, at other times, in tears or in a smoldering antagonism. What settled the rage were the stomp-and-swear walks. I'd walk miles in any direction, stomping and swearing the whole way until I ran out of bad words. Then I'd turn around and walk home. Sometimes I was three miles out. In the end, I wore myself out on it and realized that while rage needed to be expressed physically, appropriately, and with great respect for its power, it had limited applications.

My feet hurt.

When I got past rage, I was hungry for the *why* of things. There was no more surfacing. I had to go for the depths, seeking the cause of the cause of the cause, the why of the why, seven times deep, clear back to the original sources which are cultural, genetic, historical, spiritual, and physical. I followed a slippery pathway through the backwoods of my own cultural and family history, becoming fearless in the search for what was masked, what was skewed, what was shadowed.

Fact is lost over generations. Every story is second- or third-hand, guesses and projections and surmises. But it is in the piecing together of details over time that allows our lives to finally make sense. Road weary enough to know that the universe operates only on truth, I learned that nothing will move, clear, heal, or transcend until the truth of the truth is scraped bare and exposed. When that happened, when I finally hit it dead center, I felt like I'd been struck by lightning.

Over and over I was left with an almost nausea, and a sense of disorientation. Why? Because there were many truths, many stories, many whys. Yet the payoff was profound. When I finally began to understand the whys of the whys, the healing and forgiving become as easy as pulling on a pair of old socks.

Colleen, a friend with her own history of trouble, said this to me: "We're all crazy. And the only thing you can do is forgive everybody in every direction. Parents, spouses, children, family, friends. In every way, all the time, all at once."

We forgive our contrary little communities and our lunatic families. We forgive our social and cultural history. We forgive whatever gods we have to forgive and beckon them back into our lives. We forgive our own idiocy.

The night I received the surgeon's email, I felt the lightning strike, along with the disorientation and the nausea that truth brings. I realized that I was still carrying the weight of what had happened and needed to let it go as well.

"This is the developmental task of our middle years, letting go of the things that no longer serve us" said my friend, Jeanette, who'd just let go of a loveless marriage. "This one thing we do at this stage of our lives."

I had to let go of my mother's death
and breathe.
I had to let go of my father's illness
and breathe.
I had to let go of no children

and breathe
and breathe
and breathe.

I had to let go of what had happened last
and what might happen next.

And breathe.

Let go.

And walk.

And afterward? I began to clean my house, deeply, with great intention: The closets were turned out, bookshelves emptied, beds upended, the interstices scrubbed, the skeleton polished. I moved the refrigerator and scrubbed under it. I threw out old shoes, dresses a size or six too small, single socks, and yards of fabric I'd intended to make into clothing.

I'd always had a box fetish. Raised on the farm, we'd kept boxes for Christmas for mailings, for sending home goodies with friends and neighbors. It was important to hang on to a good box.

Well, I had a closet piled with empty brown boxes.

They went.

The closet had racks of empty coat hangers.

They went.

Empty purses and good brown paper sacks, you know, the kind with handles.

They went as well.

I had been hoarding emptiness.

What saves us? The answer was what I thought it might be.

My extended family watched my disintegration with a surreal patience, offering genuine help, quiet understanding, and rambunctious humor. We were a tangle of rubber bands, pulling at each other from time to time, stressing the center almost to the popping point. Somehow it held.

My blood kin helped me sift through the debris of our history and find what was worthy of revelation and, sometimes by their silences, what to leave well enough alone. They were the stabilizing force during the questioning years, quietly absorbing the bits of family history they weren't quite sure they believed, letting the questions sit as silently as the moon. Our unholy legacy stopped with my generation, and provided a pathway of greater physical and emotional health for our children and their children and their children after that. There would be no more children with muscular dystrophy in my family.

My familial matriarchs and patriarchs, whose wisdom I had to grow into, urged this wild-headed, wrong-headed self to cooperate with life as I found it, to love deeply all

the lines and tangles of family, and to not resist the goodness that was also part of our heritage. They loaned me
strength when I had none of my own.

We came through this together.

My brother often took better care of my father than I
did. In his later years, Dad lived forty miles away, and he
would call my brother and say, "I got the pneumonia." My
brother would leave work, rush him to a hospital, and then
take care of my father's home. My brother literally carried
my dad every where he went for the last fifteen years of my
father's life. Chair to wheelchair to car to wheelchair to
house, to doctor's office, to store. And back again. And
again and again.

My brother, Steve, is as strong and reliable as the Idaho
soil we came from. He is the patriarch now.

On the day I had a hysterectomy, Steve came to pick me
up, five in the morning. I crawled into the Bronco, and he
set the stereo *significantly* higher than our usual decibels,
blasting the 1812 Overture, *rendered in the honks and squeaks
of cows and chickens, dogs and sheep.* I laughed – hard laughter – all the way to the hospital. The laughter of survival.

My family saves me.

My niece, Mackenzie, and my nephew, Scott, have eyes the
color of alpine lakes, hair the color of corn silk. When
Mackenzie, this elegant child, was six years old, her grand-

mother fell and broke her arm on the sidewalk outside of daycare. Mackenzie had the presence of mind to call 911, get help, and then sit with her grandmother until the ambulance arrived. I spent the afternoon with Mackenzie after the accident and loaned her my serenity ball necklace.

"Mackenzie, do you want to keep the necklace?" I asked.

"No, I'll just wear it until my soul comes back together."

Scottie makes friends instantly. He's the child who will crawl on your lap to be hugged and held. He only wants real stories, and he recently announced to me that he learns 2,851,365 new things every day. I believe him. He decided to teach himself to read at four because "I wanna read those Hardy Boys." His giggle upends me. The world *as it is* fashions him, compels him outward.

One afternoon a few years ago, the three of us were going to see a movie. "Aunt Barb," Scott piped up from the back seat of the car. "Do you need a publisher for your book?"

"Yes, Scottie, I do," I said, wondering what the heck this kid had in mind.

"I'll publish it for you," he said.

He was seven years old.

Children heal me because they yank me out of my own skin. Macaroni and cheese must be prepared, teeth must be brushed, stories of their parents, grandparents, aunts, and uncles must be told again and again. These stories are their lodestar, the distance and direction from where they have come, the distance and direction they are to go. These stories teach them about the integrity of family, the making of mistakes and the making of amends, the finding of our peculiar pathways, the rewards of hard work, the passion for life *however it comes,* the laughter that drenches us in the magnificent. These stories must become buried deeply in the convolutions of their brains, so that they never lose their way, never forget from whence they came.

This is what aunts are for. Every night that I am with them, just before sleep, I tell them how strong, how beautiful, how smart, how kind they are. They go to sleep with the sound of their own wings swirling in their heads.

My family saves me.

The physicians at the muscular dystrophy clinic had grown fond of Pop, the old tease. They told him he was the oldest living muscular dystrophy patient on record. Maybe so. He died at the age of seventy-seven. He seldom talked of his illness to them, never, ever complained about how weak he was getting, how little control he had over his hands and arms.

"How are you doing?" they'd ask. Pop would duck his head, say, "Fine, thanks," and then regale them with the story of catching a twenty-five-pound channel cat, or the times he carried his winter meat out on his back, a trek of six miles either straight up or straight down, often in snow and subzero weather. He never made up his stories, never expanded them or exploited them.

Every time he'd go to the clinic, he'd ask "those old docs when they were going to get something to fix my back," his euphemism for his illness. They'd tell him about how the muscles were not using a particular protein, how the answer might come through genetic engineering. He was adamant in his search for clues about his illness, read everything he could, but he misconstrued the information, often famously.

Pop had been reading about gene replacement therapy for muscular dystrophy patients. He wanted to know about the possibility of gene replacement for himself.

"You know, Doc," he said. "When we get ready to do them gene replacements, I know what genes I want."

Dr. Wilson waited patiently.

"I got an old striped tomcat out by my place. I want them genes."

Late afternoon, about a month or so before my father's death, I was visiting him at the nursing home. He was sitting in his wheelchair, a thing he'd resisted fiercely until he realized he could get around on his own power again. He'd always been a hard man to hug, literally. For a long time, he'd been confined to his recliner. Now the wheelchair created the same distance, the same obstacles.

We'd had so many fights that at this stage of our lives together, we were – I think now – finally tender toward one another, two pockmarked, battle-weary warriors who had a genuine regard for each other. We still had moments of emotional spitting at each other, but they lacked any power. No more firestorms.

He was sitting in his wheelchair in front of a large window that looked toward the Boise Front, toward Bogus Basin. It was a rainy day, and the clouds curled against those hills. In his room were pictures of my niece, a painting of a trout, a portrait of his parents. His necessaries were on the window sill – aspirin, toenail clippers, a spider plant, chocolates to share with his nurses (a bribe-bait to assure that they checked on him in a timely manner). He'd always been mesmerized by his mountains, and that day he was dreaming he could still walk in them. He always trusted them. I came up and put my arms around him from the rear of his chair and he leaned his head over so he could touch my face, a tenderness we'd rarely shared. We stayed that way for a long time, maybe twenty minutes, maybe an hour, maybe an eternity.

We lost the taste for time.

My family saves me.

The afternoon my mother died, before we knew she had passed away, we were driving back to the hospital, watching the farmland go by. I do not remember very much about the days leading up to her death, and I do not remember what happened after her death.

This much I do remember. The sun was at an angle, shining through the dark and circling clouds, sifting through an afternoon thunderstorm. The extraordinary golden light came down from the sky in rays, illuminating the rows of cornstalks, leaving the silks gleaming. The light defined the bales of hay lying in straight lines in the fields, their shadows a relief against the green. The light moved across the landscape as openings in the clouds gave it force and direction, captured by dust and imagination. The light glowed through the leaves of black walnut, elm, and catalpa. The breeze caused the wheat, the color and density of jade, to bend and then straighten, the long stems and heavy heads dancing to the oldest music. The light caressed what looked like a living sea. The world was all green movement, all grace, a reminiscence of my childhood, all sweet peace.

She was dying at that very moment. That light, I'm thinking, was a promise and a warning: The clouds will be dark and foreboding, but the light will find a way, always the light will find a way.

I have stumbled half-blind through glory ever since.

My family saves me.

The family that can rend you asunder can put you back together.

For me, for this one woman at this particular time, healing came not as an intervention of the Divine, but with an interaction with the divine sweetness found in ordinary life. The divinity I found in the circling arms of my family and friends; in children who love dinosaurs and stuffed pink bears; in my parents' stories and their memories; in leaning against the mountains I've learned to trust, caressing golden rays that part the clouds long enough to set landscape on fire.

There is no more sacred journey than the trek through understanding, forgiveness, and letting go, ordinary and ancient as those requirements are.

What does this feel like?

You tend to feel sorrow over the circumstance instead of rage.... You tend to have nothing left to remember to say about it all. You understand the suffering that drove the offense to begin with. You prefer to remain outside the milieu. You are not waiting for anything. You are not wanting anything. There is no lariat snare about your ankle stretching from way back there to here. You are free to go.

—CLARISSA PINKOLA ESTES

This one thing, this letting go, was easy as the mind relaxing into something sweet, intimate, and holy. When the heart is ready, the mind easily follows. When I finally released my litany, my tangled history floated upward like the notes of a hymn.

Over ten thousand Christmas lights illuminate our local botanical garden on a snowy, subfreezing night. Our botanical garden is set back against the foothills and overlooks our city. No moon. Millions of stars. Multiplied and intensified by snow and ice, the Christmas lights surround Juanita and me. "It Came Upon A Midnight Clear" is playing softly in the background. We sip hot chocolate and wander through a magical landscape, a crystal night, the epitome of every Christmas dream I've ever had.

The gardens are perched against an ancient prison, the prison of our early days as a territory and then as a state. It carries a tawdry history. The treatment was brutal there: no heat, no sunlight, appalling food, torture. Men and women went mad there. The prison is a museum now, but its past can haunt us if we're not careful. Juanita feels a sense of evil emanating from the prison. She says it's the result of harm done to the human spirit. I trust her observation, but I leave her to wander on her own.

I turn away from the prison and look at the light that

surrounds me: Christmas light, city light, snow light, starlight.

I needed to look at a dark and foreboding past, the prisons of my own making, acknowledged in truth and power. But after that was accomplished, I needed to look in another direction, to follow my own illuminated pathways, and to move with a lighter step, free of ghosts and dark memory.

I absorb the ten thousand Christmas lights that surround me, the hundred thousand city lights at my feet, and savor the millions of lights in the night sky, coming toward me from every direction all at once.

I watch the planet as it tilts, dangerous as that might be, and relish what light there is.

Coda:

What Life Is

SUN VALLEY AT the end of May is an emanation of
sweetness. The greens are both soft and intense, and the
mountains outside the tall, slim windows of a conference
room draw our attention. The curtains are pulled back, and
the room catches and holds the glow of the mountains.
Seventy or so women and a few men are listening intently
as Judie, our local wise woman and healer, talks about the
ordinary passages in our lives. She speaks of the stages she
had learned about recently: birth, initiation, exploration,
demonstration, merging, attainment, and death. When she
reaches the description of attainment, she says this: "It's
the time of life when we no longer have to prove anything
to ourselves or anyone else. It is a remarkably peaceful,
transcendent passage."

She asks the audience if anyone has achieved this stage of life. A tiny woman behind me raises her hand. "Will you stand and tell us a bit about your feelings?" Judie asks. The woman, who appears to be a rather frail late-fifties, perhaps early-sixties woman, has soft curling brown hair, a wealth of wrinkles – sun damage from gardening, I'm thinking. She stands tentatively and says, "God always provides. You can trust that. I'm always happy."

We sigh, not quite comfortable with such a platitude, such an easy answer.

A young woman across the room jumps up and says, "Bessie, you have to tell them how old you are."

"I'm eighty-six."

The audience claps and laughs, their perceptions shaken.

The younger woman explains, "Bessie and my mother, and a few other women, have been friends for over sixty years. They've lived adventurous lives, physically and intellectually and spiritually. They supported each other through births and marriages, divorces and death. They've had children, grandchildren, and great-grandchildren. They've grown their own organic food since the 1930s. They've practiced massage and taken vitamins since their twenties. They gave each of us *Bhagavad Gita* to read when we were twenty years old, which altered our perceptions considerably, as you can imagine. They still travel together. Their next trip: Istanbul."

A globe-trotting great-grandmother who lived holisti-
cally seventy years before it was fashionable is telling us
that great happiness comes toward the end of life and that
we could trust God. It is an astonishing peek at bliss.

"Life is what it is," Bessie says, "It takes a gratitude for it."

About the Author

Barbara Herrick is a poet, an essayist, and a glory-years woman. Her work ranges in topic from Shakespeare to the Egyptians and has appeared in local, regional, and national magazines. Barbara is a voracious reader and has a passion for knitting, cooking for others, and Belgian chocolate. She is also the author of two coffee-table books on Boise, Idaho, where she makes her home with family, friends, and her Maine Coon cat, Paxter – a mop with attitude.

You can find Barbara's website at
www.blackberryteaclub.com.

To Our Readers

CONARI PRESS, an imprint of Red Wheel/Weiser, publishes books on topics ranging from spirituality, personal growth, and relationships to women's issues, parenting, and social issues. Our mission is to publish quality books that will make a difference in people's lives — how we feel about ourselves and how we relate to one another. We value integrity, compassion, and receptivity, both in the books we publish and in the way we do business.

Our readers are our most important resource, and we value your input, suggestions, and ideas about what you would like to see published. Please feel free to contact us, to request our latest book catalog, or to be added to our mailing list.

Conari Press
An imprint of Red Wheel/Weiser, LLC
P.O. Box 612
York Beach, ME 03910-0612
www.conari.com